# Career Talk

Everything

**You Need to Know**

to  Have a Great Career

2ND EDITION

*by Andre J. Castillo*

# Contents

INTRODUCTION ............................................4

CHAPTER 1: Good vs. Great .....................7

Find your Center ..............................13

CHAPTER 2: *Strengths*, What do I do? ...............26

CHAPTER 3: *Opportunity*, What's in it for me? ........38

How to get hired ...............................46

How to get promoted ......................50

Win all the awards ..........................58

CHAPTER 4: *Passion*, Who am I? ....................67

CHAPTER 5: The Plan .......................78

How do I switch to an entirely new career? ........93

CHAPTER 6: The Routine .....................98

CHAPTER 7: Do I need a mentor? ................108

CHAPTER 8: Health ....................115

CHAPTER 9: How can I save a lot of time? ............125

CHAPTER 10: How do I write a great resume? ......134

How do I write a cover letter?...................... 146

CHAPTER 11: How do I ace my interview?........... 149

Public speaking................................ 158

CHAPTER 12: Should I network? Online?............. 164

The importance of flattery ..................... 176

Optimizing your LinkedIn presence ................ 178

Your online reputation ......................... 180

CHAPTER 13: Going (back) to school.................... 187

How to get A's when you need them:
*The Test-the-Test Method* ......................... 188

How to get into Harvard ........................ 199

Law school: think twice ........................ 204

Master's degree: think thrice ................... 206

PhD: Highest of its Kind......................... 207

CHAPTER 14: What if…........................................ 209

What if I want to be an artist? .................. 210

What if I'm a woman? Or a minority?............. 213

CHAPTER 15: Leadership ..................................... 219

CONCLUSION: Beware the Uncanny Valley .......... 235

# Introduction

My father grew up in Los Angeles so poor that for one birthday his cake was a piece of toast with a candle on it. He didn't know what he wanted to be when he grew up until one Christmas day when he was 8 years old, police officers came to his house. Not for a citation, not for an arrest — they came to give him a *toy car*. And you know what my father became when he grew up? *A police officer*. Before long, my father had joined the U.S. Air Force and received the training he needed, became a police officer, and moved back to a comfortable middle class life in California where for his entire adult life he volunteered to give back to other, less fortunate children in his community.

My father's story as I described it revolves around his career. This is not unusual whenever we tell stories – the stories of our lives are inextricably bound to the fates of our careers. Our careers are incredibly important to us. I'm sure you recognize that your career is important too, but if you asked yourself right now, I bet you might say that your family is more important. Or your faith, or community. And I would agree with you, in the grand scheme of things they are more important. But think – how likely are you to support a family without a good job? Or to support your church or community if you are in debt, unemployed, or miserable? The very things that we care about most suffer, or are even unattainable, if your career pulls you down financially, or emotionally, or if it pulls you to a location that rips you away from what you care about. While in the moral sense your career is not as important as these other aspects of your life, in a logistical sense it very much is.

Think of a time when you were forced to do something you hated, whether it was a chore for your parents, a personal errand, or a task at work. How did you feel? Did you slump your shoulders? Did you have less energy, get sick a little more? Maybe a lot more? Now imagine feeling that every day. For the rest of your life. How horrible would that be? And yet it's happening to many, many people right this very second.

*Career Talk* is a tool for you to do more than just avoid that outcome. It's a tool for you to be that inspiration, that toy car, for your own career and the careers of another generation in your community. Instead of being geared to 8 year olds, of course, this book is much more advanced, and is aimed to the adults and teenagers that are living through today's tough job market.

I'm a former Presidential Management Fellow, Alumni and Dean Scholar, and an award-winning public servant and public speaker. I have led and consulted for great career programs. I've been admitted great academic programs, including Harvard Law and Johns Hopkins University, where I earned my Master's degree. You can trust me when I say that I can help you and those you work with, manage, and care about.

I provide in-person career counseling as one of my many professional roles, and at the end of my sessions people would always ask me, Andre — Where do you get all of this great advice? And how do I find this advice too? And I would say — it's easy, just read these 30 books that I've read from the best experts in the world! That's all you need to do!

I had no idea how discouraging I sounded. They needed help *now*, I discovered, they didn't have time to read and do everything that I did over 10 years as a part of my career. So instead, I took all of those books, and the hundreds and hundreds of articles, biographies, podcasts, and success stories that I use to teach others as a career development expert and instead I put all of those resources into this one book.

Now you don't have to read every website and every book that talks about careers, and try to separate what really works from what doesn't, because *Career Talk* does that for you. It gives you that foundation.

## Acknowledgements

I had a lot of help learning everything that went into this book, and in writing it. First and foremost thank you to my beautiful wife and editor-in-chief, Hannah, for helping me test all of these ideas (before we even started dating!) and for being so excited to see the finished product, which provided me motivation to no end. Thank you to the following contributors: my bestest man and mentor Shawn Mohamed, James Parent, Mark Gibson, Erica Hilton, Vince Pereira, Dan Jackson, Dustin Canter, Liz Bohannon, Corey Jackson, Will Hopkins, Ileana Galvan, Sammy Chester, Nathan Hitchen, Anthony Zitkus, Glenn Ellmers, Dr. Matt Deaton, and Mr. Joe Nunez. And a deep thank you to *all* of my mentors and teachers along the way, including Ed Berman and Al Karnig for teaching me how to write properly in the first place; to Ralph Salmi for teaching me how to research (and listen) properly; to Pam Langford, Brian Janiskee, David Yaghoubian, Dany Doueiri, Nicole Cowley, Juan Regalado, and Mike McKenzie for their early career advice and support when I needed it most; to my SAIS advisors Camille Pecastaing and the late, great Fouad Ajami for showing me what it truly takes to write a great book; and to my career mentors John Sepúlveda and Armando Rodriguez, who always went out of their way to set me up for career success, a debt I can never repay enough. And of course, thank you to my amazing family for *everything*. To my mom, dad, Noel, Tyler, and all 100+ members of my extended family – this is for you! (No seriously, Tyler, this really is for you; you really do need to read this book!)

# CHAPTER 1

## Good vs. Great

*Good is the enemy of the great. And that is one of the key reasons why we have so little that becomes great. We don't have great schools, principally because we have good schools. We don't have great government, principally because we have good government. Few people attain great lives, in large part because it is just so easy to settle for a good life. The vast majority of companies never become great, precisely because the vast majority become quite good – and that is their main problem.[1] – Jim Collins, author of Good to Great: Why Some Companies Make the Leap…and Others Don't*

As Jim Collins wrote in his 2001 best seller, every day we settle for good when we can be great. We do this for many reasons. We know that we can't be great at everything, so we don't try to be. It's impossible. I'm not a great poker player, but I'm a good one, and I'm happy with that. I'm also not a great basketball player – and I definitely, *never* will be. But I did achieve something in basketball. My wife thinks I'm a good player. And do you think hearing her say that made me happy? You bet it did. Most of the time, being good *enough* is just fine.

But I do like to think that I am great at something. I don't think that I am a good employee, for example. I honestly believe that I'm a great one. I've won numerous awards throughout my life and have glowing references, whether they are from people that I have managed, colleagues or directors and executives that I have worked with, or from the many people I have coached to achieving their career goals. Here is one story from a reader of this very book:

> *What stood out to me while reading* Career Talk *was the topic of passion. I had lost that, and I knew my attitude was one of the main reasons I had been passed over for several promotions. I decided to resign, accepting that I had blown those opportunities, and I put my resume out so I could start new somewhere else. I was hired elsewhere and I gave my two week notice. During those two weeks, I reignited my passion, figuring I better start living it now instead of waiting for the new job. That caught management's attention. On the third day before I was to leave, I was asked what it would take to keep me with the firm. I was given the promotion and increase in my salary that I had sought. Later, I asked another manager from a different department why it took my resignation to finally get that promotion, and he told me that had had nothing to do with it. It was the way I had approached my exit. He told me, "You showed a passion about everything you were doing, and management didn't want that walking out the door."*

My proudest achievement came very recently – in late 2014 my team unveiled a new version of a web-based career development program that trains 80,000 people to achieve their career goals per month. I'll always look back and believe the resulting product, MyCareer@VA 2.0, was great. To me, that makes all the difference. Creating that site – a project that involved an amazing team that I relied on to build, a site that helps and trains tens of thousands of people every month – was a constant struggle. I had to fight for that site and its program almost every day. So many times it looked like the end result would not even be good, let alone great – I was told more than once that the whole thing would have to shut down – and overcoming those pressures was the single most challenging thing I have ever done in my career – or to my hair, which is thinner and grayer than ever.

And I've never been happier. I helped create something that I can be proud of for the rest of my life, a product that will help thousands, perhaps even millions of people. This matters. My career isn't just what I do – it's how I met my wife, it's how I bought my home, and it's how I help others every day. Our careers are the foundation, the wellspring, of everything that we do and are. And if we get that part right, everything else in life becomes that much easier as well.

Now, I want you to think of a time, any time, when it felt like you did something great, no matter how big or how small, whether in your personal life or your professional life. Throughout this book we're going to talk about what it is that leads us to produce those moments of greatness that you're thinking of right now – and how you can set yourself up to make your entire career go from good *enough* to great.

### What does it mean to be great? The 80-20 Rule

In the late 1800's, Italian economist Vilfredo Pareto noticed something interesting in his garden, where he grew peas. In his garden, Pareto observed that nearly all of his peas, about 80% of them, came from just a handful of his pea pods – just 20% of those. In other words, 20% of Pareto's pea pods were making 80% of his peas – far more than their fair share. Inspired by this fact he went on to observe similar relationships in the Italian economy, most famously that 80% of Italy's land at the time was owned by just 20% of Italy's population. From there, this effect – now known as the 80-20 Rule – has been observed in virtually every field, from business, to science, to computing and communications. 80% of computer errors come from 20% of the bugs. 80% of a company's complaints come from 20% of its customers. 80% of a company's profits come from 20% of its customers or 20% of its staff (or, even, 20% of its staff's time).

So what does this mean for you? *You are after that 80%.* No matter how small your work group or your project, you as an individual – or your team, organization, or your company – can vastly out produce your competitors, with even *less effort* than they put in as a whole. You can actually measure this to give you a benchmark to strive for. Allow me to illustrate.

### *The Greatness Equation:* How do I know if I'm great?

We're going to use some numbers to help you figure out whether you are in the good or great category at any given time. First let's restate our premise:

1. *Am I good?* ➜    *I am one of the 80% of people accomplishing 20% of the results.*

2. *Am I **great?*** ➜    *I am one of the **20%** of people accomplishing **80%** of the results.*

Next, let's measure it. For this example, we'll say you are in a work group with four other people, and as a group you are, total, supposed to produce 20 "widgets" ("widgets" can be anything – training classes, sales, reports, computer programs, etc.). Knowing what we know about the 80-20 Rule, in this scenario, **how many widgets does each employee make?** See if you can figure it out on your own.

The correct answer is that there is *one great employee who will make 16 widgets* and each of the other four good employees will make 1 widget each. In other words, as a general rule:

**A great employee is <u>16 times</u> as productive as the average employee!**[*]

That's the answer. You can be **16 times as productive** as the average employee. Not only that, but there is no real known exception to this rule. In fact, if anything, this example I provided *understates* the relationship – in various instances the 80-20 is rule has actually been measured to be a 90-10 rule, or even a 99-1 rule. So remember:

❖ If you work alone, you can be 16 times as effective as the average employee in your field.

❖ If you work in a team, your team can be 16 times as effective as the average team.

❖ If you work in a company, your company can be 16 times as effective as the average company.

And so on. There are other benchmarks for other fields as to what it means to be great that you will need to learn on your own (I personally don't use the 80-20 Rule to assess every single project I do), but the 80-20 Rule is the simplest and most universal rule of thumb of what it means to be great, which is why I use it here. You can use this benchmark to strive for greatness in your field. That is why it is so useful. You can *plan* to achieve this goal of being 16 times better than the average. Here's how.

## The Hedgehog Concept

---

[*] If you're curious, here's the math: 5 people make 20 widgets. Applying the 80-20 Rule to your 5 people in the work group translates to 1 great employee (20%) and 4 good employees (80%). Now apply 80-20 to your widgets. That translates to 16 widgets made by the great employee (80%) and 4 widgets made by the good employees (20%): 16 widgets per great employee and 1 widget per good employee.

How to go from good to great can be explained in one simple diagram, composed of three circles.

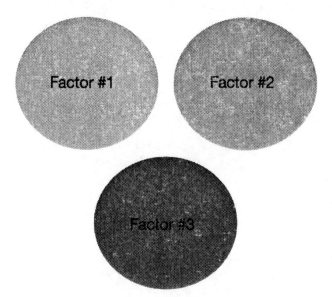

This is what Jim Collins calls The Hedgehog Concept. Collins first discovered this concept in the bestseller he co-wrote with Jerry Porras, *Built to Last*, which studied 18 historically great companies and what made them so successful. Years later, Collins studied 11 different companies that did not begin as great companies but instead "made the leap" to greatness after years of mediocrity, in his follow up entitled *Good to Great*. In both books, Collins found that the most successful companies throughout history consistently followed the concept, while their competitors did not.

Where these three circles overlap is where these companies found greatness – and so will you. I call this your **Center**.

## Find your Center

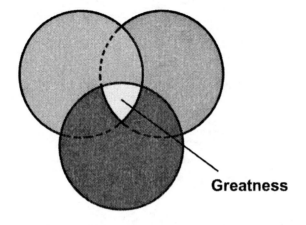

**Greatness**

But before we can know where these three circles overlap – your Center – we have to know what resides in each circle, and what that means for you. Think for a moment to see if you can figure them out on your own.

Now, I want you to think of that time when you "felt" that you had done something great. What was different about this project compared to the others, why do you think you were able to make it great? Where was your Center? Keep thinking about that great thing you did, but now, ask yourself would what happen to that great thing if we took away:

Your skill?

What if you weren't good at the tasks you had to do? Would your project still have been great?

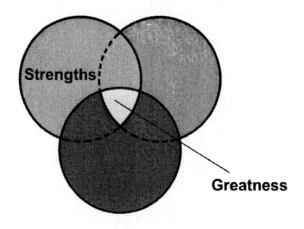

### Warren Buffet's secret

Warren Buffett is perhaps the world's most successful investor, and one of the richest men in the world. He has made his fortune from astutely observing which companies will succeed, which will not, and investing accordingly. In the 1970's and again in the 1980's, American banks were wracked with crises, with many banks losing money or failing entirely. Warren Buffet was among the many skeptics of the banking industry at the time, yet in 1989 he chose to invest $290 million into one particular bank – Wells Fargo – despite his overall pessimism towards the banking industry. And sure enough, Wells Fargo has gone from being worth just $1 a share in 1989 to $55 a share today. During the period that Jim Collins studied Wells Fargo, Wells Fargo produced stock returns four times higher than the average return for the entire banking industry. It was the best of its class, and Warren Buffet made a lot of money on that $290 million investment.

Explaining his rationale, Buffet said: "They stick with what they understand and let their abilities, not their egos, determine what they attempt."[2] Wells Fargo played to its strengths – what it could be best at. According to Collins:

> Prior to clarifying its Hedgehog Concept, Wells Fargo had tried
> to be a global bank...and a mediocre one at that. Then...Wells

*Fargo executives began to ask themselves a piercing set of questions: What can we potentially do better than any other company, and, equally important, what can we not do better than any other company? And if we can't be the best at it, then why are we doing it at all?*

*Putting aside their egos, the Wells Fargo team pulled the plug on the vast majority of its international operations, accepting the truth that it could not be better than Citicorp in global banking. Wells Fargo then turned its attention to what it could be the best in the world at: running a bank like a business, with a focus on the western United States. That's it. That was the essence of the Hedgehog Concept that turned Wells Fargo from a mediocre Citicorp wanna-be to one of the best-performing banks in the world.*[3]

Like Wells Fargo, you too cannot do anything great without playing to your strengths, and you must understand what those are. What your strengths are will be discussed more in the chapter on strengths. Before we get there however let's see what is in that second circle. Thinking back to your great accomplishment – like Wells Fargo, you had to have *some* amount of skill, there's no way you could have succeeded if you were absolutely terrible at the task at hand. And the more skill you had, the better for the end result. Now, what if you kept your strengths, but we took away:

Your opportunity?

What if, for example, your resources, your funding, or time, were taken away at the time you were meant to accomplish that great thing?

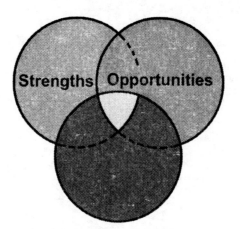

In 2012, I created a new internship program for the federal government. The reviews were stellar. My favorite review came from one of my star interns who followed up her internship in my program with one at the White House, possibly the most prestigious internship in the world. By the time she was done with school she had also completed internships at the Department of Homeland Security and the news agencies ABC and NBC. Of all those internship programs, she said *my* program was by far the best. [†]

Just as suddenly as the program had taken off, by 2013 it had closed. New federal regulations had come out that completely changed the way we could recruit interns, the key component of the program. The entire program had been built on the old system, and when the new system arrived, it could not adapt. The program I built and loved could no longer function. And just like that, the opportunity for that great program had come to an end.

I tell this story because it is very easy to think of other closed windows all around us, but the real truth is that there are opportunities for greatness all around us, every day. It wasn't long before I was working on bigger, more impactful programs, where I

---

[†] The program made such a good impression of me on her, that two years later we were married.

could use my strengths even more than I did before. It didn't happen right away however. I started with smaller opportunities; for months after that program had effectively ended, instead of (solely) trying to revive my program, I hunted and latched on to a small opportunity here, another there, knowing that I needed to continue to make a positive impact not only for my career, but for my sanity. Even with a moribund program I still saw opportunities for greatness.

So what did I do? I volunteered to create a web site, a web-based system that our office could use to manage their many large programs and projects. I wasn't required to make it, it wasn't my job – I didn't even really know how to do it when I volunteered to – I just knew that I *could* learn how to do it quick enough and well enough that I could make a real positive impact. In other words, I saw the opportunity, one that aligned with my strengths in learning new technology and processes, and I pitched the idea to my boss.

My boss said yes to my pitch, and people liked my project so much that when another large web-based program had an opening – which just so happened to be a great career development program – I was the first person my office thought of to lead it, so I was appointed to run it. I ended up effecting more positive change in the first year I ran that program than in all of the previous years of my career combined. It was a great, unexpected opportunity – but one that I earned through the good will of smaller, completely voluntary opportunities that I took advantage of first.

Now think about all of the opportunities you have today, in and outside of work.

Think broadly. What is there to stop you from having a great day, today? Or being a great parent, a great friend, a great neighbor, a great mentor, a great employee, or a great leader? As you will learn in the chapter on opportunity, these are all opportunities to be great on any given day, and any one of them can help lead you to a great career. Of course you can't be great at all of these opportunities every day, but couldn't you be great at one of these on one day? Or on most days? Or be great at a couple of these, every single day? *That* is what you want to be asking yourself.

Opportunity is the second circle. You can also think of it as the *What's In It For Me?* circle.

### How good-to-great companies view opportunity

How many of those 11 good-to-great companies that Collins studied do you think were in great industries that had lots of opportunities in front of them? Industries that were just exploding in money, like how the tech industry has exploded in the past few years? You would probably think that it's important to be in a great industry to be successful, and that a majority of these companies were in great industries. You would be wrong.

Just *one* of those good-to-great companies was in a "great" industry that was exploding with growth, opportunity, and cash. Nearly half of the great companies were in industries that were actually losing money overall, yet those companies still became great. This is because there are opportunities for greatness everywhere – even in bad industries – if you just know how to look for them.

The term that Collins uses here to describe what I'm calling opportunity is "Your Economic Engine." In private industry, one of your keys to success has to be making money – if you can't make money, if you can't pay your employees, your company will wither and die. Because of this, the great companies that he studied were not only great at understanding what they could do well at, they were also very innovative in determining what was the best way for them to make money. This is what Collins calls their "economic denominator." In other words, if you can't be paid or rewarded for it in some way, it's not much of an opportunity, is it? Think of it as the bottom line – *What's in it for you*?

When it comes to your career, you probably think of your bottom line in terms of salary and benefits (results) and long hours worked (inputs). If so, you would be similar to the average companies from Collins's study – profits were most important to them, so that's what they measured. But what Collins's study reveals is that not everyone gets his or her bottom line right. The book is littered with examples of companies that failed to align their bottom line with the actual opportunities that were in front of them – they focused so much on simplistic, traditional measurements that they failed to take advantage of opportunities that would *lead* them to making more money in the long term.

When it comes to your career, you will have opportunities of many kinds, not just salary and benefits but to produce results, win awards and garner recognition from creating new projects, boost your productivity by learning new skills, and enhance your network or reputation – each of which can directly improve your resume and chance for an interview or a promotion, or just flat out make you happier on the job. When it comes to opportunities always keep in mind what it is you are "measuring" your own success with, and never forget that you will get what you measure. If you choose to measure something that cannot actually produce greatness in your field – like working the longest hours, which tends to result in less sleep and shoddier work – you will then be mediocre. The best opportunities may be something else entirely – perhaps how many people you can meet (networking), how many people you can help (creating projects), or how many training courses you can take (learning skills).

Whenever you learn something new about your environment – see a new article on Twitter, hear your boss talking about the future of the company – ask yourself, is there an *opportunity* here? If so, make a note and circle back to it and see if it fits into your Center. And if it does, make a plan to act on it as soon as possible.

Now, let's go back to that great accomplishment of yours one more time. What if we still gave you your skills, and we still gave you your opportunity (i.e. your time and resources), but we took away:

Your passion?

What if I waved a magic wand and said that the great project you were working on – you were still very skilled, you did have the resources you needed – but now, you don't care about it anymore? You care about something else. What effect do you think that would have?

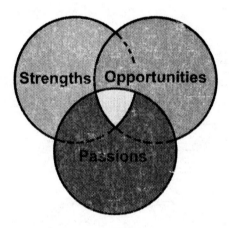

One year in graduate school, I volunteered to spend my spring break building composting latrines in a rural Panamanian village that had no access to sanitary water or electricity. In other words, I volunteered to spend my vacation building toilets. I'll never forget the look on the faces of my friends and family when I would tell them this story and how excited I was; the look they gave me made me feel like I was a zoo animal, and not the cute kind. I couldn't understand why they weren't as excited as I was. The experience taught me what it means to have passion.

The composting latrines I helped build in rural Panama were so much more to me, and to those Panamanians, than toilets. This village already had toilets – outhouses built alongside the creek that ran through the village and supplied it with water. But these outhouses were extremely unsanitary. Not only did they smell and attract insects, they leaked into the soil and into the creek as well. This made the creek water very dangerous to drink, particularly for non-locals who did not build up a tolerance to its bacteria. My team could not drink the water – we had to purchase bottled water from a town hours away and drive it into the village. Not only did the composting latrines solve this problem for the homes we could afford to build them for – by preventing the runoff into the soil and into the creek – true to their name, they also produced compost that the residents could use to fertilize their crops. My team of volunteers and I literally sweat and bled to assemble the requisite wire, gravel, cement and concrete.

All of the people I interacted with were wonderful – my team and the locals alike – and in just one week we built something that will marginally improve their lives for years to come. And I loved every minute of it. I will cherish those memories forever.

And that is how I learned that I am truly passionate about helping others. I will do anything to help others – even if it means building toilets. And I will enjoy every single minute of it. And others will look at me like I'm absolutely nuts when I tell them about it.

Writer Paul Graham tells a story of how he asked his father, a mathematician, about his interest in math. "Didn't it get boring?" he asked his father. "No," his father replied. For Paul, math was *work*, something he forced himself to do that he didn't enjoy. But to his father, they were fun problems to be solved. For his father, the math problems at the end of his math book were a reward, and he would rush to finish them whenever he received a new test book – long before his teacher ever assigned them.[4]

Like the younger Paul doing math problems, I'm sure you know very well what it's like to not be passionate about a task at hand. Your shoulders slump a bit, you move slower, you can't help but look at the clock, your lunch breaks become cause for celebration, and your Fridays – those hallowed occasions – become so profound you might even celebrate *Friday Eve*. Lacking passion is profoundly limiting.

Passion is so important that the good-to-great companies would transform themselves in order to obtain it, even if they could hardly explain what "it" is, or why. Jim Collins writes:[5]

> *The good-to-great companies did not say, "Okay, folks, let's get passionate about what we do"... [No, they] went the other way entirely: We should only do those things that we can get passionate about.*

Consider the company Gillette:

> *When Gillette executives made the choice to build sophisticated, relatively expensive shaving systems rather than fight a low-margin battle with disposables, they did so in large part because they just couldn't get excited about cheap disposable razors.*

Or Kimberly-Clark:

> *Kimberly-Clark executives made the shift to paper-based consumer products in large part because they could get more passionate about them. As one executive put it, the traditional paper products are okay, "but they just don't have the charisma of a diaper."*

Gillette just liked higher quality razors more. Kimberly-Clark just liked diapers more. These weren't just "things" to them. They cared about them. They wanted to work on them. They wanted to help create them. Unlike these products, passion is not something that you can simply create. Instead, it is something you must discover, and then align your career choices accordingly. If you look carefully, though, I will bet you that you can find things that you are passionate about in the most unsuspecting of places.

Sadly, people often fail to achieve passion in their careers because they misunderstand passion for social status, or a job title. They obtain a career that is respectable but they don't end up practicing that which they actually care most about. There are too many lawyers that don't care for law, too many politicians that don't care for their communities, too many doctors that don't care about their patients, too many teachers that don't care about their lessons, and so on, and so on. This is not necessarily their fault – they probably did what they were told to do, and truly believed that these occupations were the right choice for them, never realizing what their true passions were, how important they were to their success, or how to incorporate them into their daily work once they were hired. As I have learned through my years of working in career development, the unfortunate truth is many people do not understand themselves or their careers well enough to make these connections. They project themselves to be something they are not, because they think that is the right thing to do. Whether due to being raised with stifled ways of thinking or lacking access to good training – or simply not aware of public training available to them – many do not have the knowledge or tools to do so.

When this happens, the results can be quite catastrophic. If you find yourself in the position of not caring for your trade, you have doomed yourself not only to mediocrity, but likely also to the scorn of those you were intended to serve. How many catastrophes, how many lives lost, have been caused by people working in jobs they were ill suited for, ones that did not fit into their own Center? I'm sure you can think of several. I can think of many.

Keep in mind that this circle doesn't mean that you have to be passionate about the specific method of doing your work. You can be passionate about writing and not be especially fond of typing, for example. You can also do writing as a part of your job without being passionate for it, as long as you are passionate about what your company stands for.[6] Or what *you* stand for.

You can be a great teacher without being passionate about everything you teach, if you are passionate about something else relevant to teaching, such as helping your students learn. And the converse is true – maybe you have students that refuse to learn the material, you can still be a great teacher if you are incredibly passionate about the material itself. If you're not passionate about the material you can still be passionate about the people, and if you're not passionate about the people you can be passionate about the material. Passion in this sense works in many ways; it can work either way. Make it work for you.

In addition to discovering your true passions, you can, and must, also enhance the passion that you already know you have. This subject will be discussed in greater length in the chapter on passion.

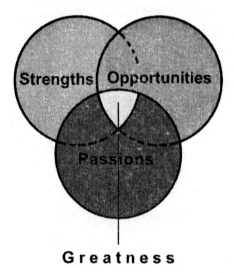

**G r e a t n e s s**

### Strengths, Opportunity, Passion – and Data

For more than ten years the non-profit institution known as the Partnership for Public Service has analyzed the federal workforce, which is comprised of more than 4 million people. According to their data, after leadership[‡],  the two biggest drivers of employee satisfaction are:[7]

- ❖ The connection between the employee's skills and the organization's mission. (Strengths and Passion)

- ❖ The employee's pay. (Opportunity)

Strengths, passion, and opportunity. Those are, statistically, what it takes to have a great, satisfying career.

---

[‡] Employee opinions of leadership is a catch-all question, what could be called a "lagging indicator." Leaders that oversee organizations that align their employees' strengths, opportunities, and passions will be more popular than leaders that don't. In other words, ask an employee what they think of their organization's leadership and they will tell you what they think of their job, and vice versa. Still, be aware that poor management can harm your career, and avoid it when you can.

# CHAPTER 2

## Strengths:

## What do I do?

*Hide not your talents. They for use were made. What's a sundial in the shade? – Benjamin Franklin*

Mary is a writer, and a good one at that. But she's not much of a talker, unlike Greg. Greg loves to chat with anyone and everyone who strolls by the office. But ask Greg to turn a report in under a deadline? Well, good luck; Mary is your go-to person for that.

One day they are assigned a new manager, Blake, who comes in and notices that on average the office is good, but not great, at filing its reports and welcoming new clients as they walk in. So Blake sends them all to training. Mary will get training in greeting clients, and Greg will get training for report writing. But this only makes Mary and Greg miserable. Mary's stomach ties into knots as she has to work through a stammer she has had since she was a child. And Greg, not the fastest typist or the best with numbers, ends up working late hours to desperately try to complete – and correct – his reports under the manager's demanding new schedule. Mary and Greg are unhappy and losing confidence fast – and considering looking for new jobs.

The story of Mary and Greg is all too common. In fact, the majority of Americans say that they don't use their strengths throughout the day. If you are Hispanic, you are less likely to use your strengths than other ethnic groups, and in terms of income, the less you make, the less likely you are to use your strengths as well.[1]

As Gallup has observed, focusing on people's weaknesses causes them to lose confidence, while focusing on their strengths does just the opposite. Gallup's studies have shown that, "people experience significant gains in self-confidence after taking StrengthsFinder and learning more about their strengths."[2] And higher self-confidence has tremendous repercussions for your future.

The higher degree of confidence that can come from learning and investing in your strengths has been shown to improve your long-term earnings and even your health. The University of Florida's Tim Judge led a 25-year study of 7,660 people. Those in the study were asked in 1979 what their level of self-confidence was. Those who said they had high self-confidence all the way back in 1979 reported significantly higher income and satisfaction with their careers 25 years later, in 2004:[3]

> The people who had more confidence in their abilities at a young age (between 14 and 22) started off with slightly higher income levels – making, on average (in 1979) $3,496 more per year than the low-confidence group. As each year went by, this gap continued to widen. When the researchers reviewed follow-up studies from 2004, the group with higher self-confidence was making $12,821 more annually compared to the average income for the lower self-confidence group.

The health differences were even more striking. According to Gallup:[4]

> When asked about the number of health problems they have that interfere with their work, the group with low self-confidence in 1979 reported almost three times as many health problems 25 years later in 2004. Almost unbelievably, the group with high-self evaluations in 1979 reported having fewer health problems in 2004 than they did 25 years before.

> The results of this study suggest that people who are aware of their strengths and build self-confidence at a young age may reap a "cumulative advantage" that continues to grow over a lifetime...Our research time found that people who had the opportunity to use their strengths early on (between the ages of 15-23) had significantly higher job satisfaction and income levels 26 years later.

### Where strengths come from

Your strengths are uniquely derived from the biological development of your brain. Learning is conducted in your brain by synapses, which transmit the information that you learn to neurons that store them and make them useful. Your synapses are so integral to the learning process that experiments have shown them to effectively "light up" as new memories are formed.

You would think that since synapses are so important to learning, you would get more of them as you became older and smarter. But you would be wrong. You actually have far more synapses at the age of six than you do as an adult.

The National Research Council describes synapse formation like an artist would describe a sculpture. Classical artists would begin with a large block of marble, carefully chiseling away bits of marble until they achieved the sculpted figure they desired. Likewise, studies of animals reveal a similar process of "pruning" for the synapses in your brain. Initially, the nervous system creates a large number of synapse connections. As the brain experiences life, the network selects the connections it deems most appropriate and removes the rest. The final product is like a sculpted work of art that constitutes, "the sensory and perhaps the cognitive bases for the later phases of [neural] development."[5]

In other words, as you age your brain becomes more and more specialized. You learn not simply by acquiring more and more "real-estate" across your neural world, but by building a higher and higher "skyscraper" on top of your pre-existing knowledge, or synapses. This is why learning foreign languages can be so much more difficult for adults than for children, and why children have much more vivid imaginations than do adults.

The paper goes on to explain that adults can still acquire limited amounts of new synapses, in effect building adjoining neural "condos" and "townhouses" next to and around the towering neural skyscraper you've already built in your brain. Think of your brain as more Roman than Mongol – an organization that starts with a highly developed (civilized) core that, gradually but surely, expands itself by conquering and civilizing the neighboring territories around it.

## The theory of comparative advantage

It is important to keep in mind that, just like greatness, your strengths are relative. You may be a fantastic football quarterback, but if you're only the second best quarterback on your team, you aren't going to be playing very much. Conversely, you could be an average quarterback and a great wide receiver, but if no one else on your team can throw the ball, you're going to be your team's quarterback, and not the team's receiver, because the quarterback position is more important. For your team, switching you from your strength (wide receiver) to their position of need (quarterback) is a good thing for them, though it may or *may not* be the best for you.

In economics, this concept is known as the theory of comparative advantage. This theory was originally coined to explain why countries like the United States import goods that it knows very well how to produce, like, say, electronic devices. The simple answer is this: while the U.S. is absolutely better at *producing* electronics than countries like China, it has an even greater comparative advantage in *designing* electronics. So while the U.S. is better at both producing and designing, it is comparatively better at *designing*. The result is that the U.S. in a sense "delegates" production to China so that the U.S. gets to focus more on its relative strength – design. What does this mean? Well, when you perform the economic analysis, what happens is the U.S. becomes much richer overall by specializing in its strengths. The U.S. gets paid more income for design work than production work, since it is relatively more valuable. And since China is able to produce electronics cheaper than the U.S., the U.S. also gets to purchase (import) electronics from China at a lower cost as well. Higher income plus lower cost of goods means playing to its strengths is a big win for the U.S. economy.

But as you get deeper into the U.S. economy, not every American, or every American city or state, has a relative strength in design. Some parts of the U.S. will still produce electronic devices because *they* have a relative strength there. They are an exception to this overall strength for the U.S.

Just like every city and state has a different comparative advantage, every person is different and has to figure out what his or her relative strengths are. You may actually need to switch from one strength to another depending on your environment. Sometimes your environment plays well for your best strengths, and – like the talented second-string quarterback who transfers to a new school to get more playing time – sometimes it does not. Sometimes you need to move somewhere else entirely – to a new job, a new office, a new company, a new location – to be able to get the most out of your strengths and your career.

### How to assess your strengths

Assessing your strengths is very simple if you're willing to invest $9.99 in yourself. (And if you're not willing to, well, let's just be honest with each other – you should stop wasting your time with this book and start lowering your expectations for your career.)

❖ First, invest in yourself by taking Gallup's online StrengthsFinder test. It is the best of its kind in helping you discover what you can be best at. The accompanying book (which I also recommend, but is optional) says you have five traits that you can be better at than at least 15,000 other people. But before you can be better than those 15,000 other people – you need to know what those strengths are, and then you need to train yourself in them. The test costs $9.99 (which you will make back easily, trust me. And no, I don't make any money when you take this test, although I really should!).*

---

* Go here to access the test: https://www.gallupstrengthscenter.com/Purchase/en-US/Product

❖ Second, use the free "Career Fit Tool" on the MyCareer@VA website[†] to see what kinds of careers it says would be a "good fit" for you. The test can give you ideas of what kinds of jobs play to your strengths. Strongly consider it since it can help you think of careers or projects that you may have never thought of. It doesn't cover every kind of career you might consider, but it does cover many, and it only takes a few minutes of your time.

## Training and development

Once you know your strengths, you need to turn them into *skills* through training and development. There are three ways to ways to do this (see if you can guess which is most important):

❖ *Formal instruction.* This includes training courses and reading.

❖ *From other people.* This includes learning from your boss and coworkers.

❖ *Working on difficult assignments.* Also known as on-the-job (OTJ) training.

The answer according to Morgan McCall, Michael M. Lombardo, and Robert W. Eichinger, and the Center for Creative Leadership (CCL) is this:

❖ 10% of successful career learning comes from training and reading (formal instruction).

❖ 20% comes from other people.

❖ *70% of learning comes from difficult, on-the-job experiences.*

Keep this in mind whenever you want to learn and develop your skills. Formal instruction is very important, as is learning from others, *but nothing is more important than just trying and doing it*

---

[†] You can access it at the following link: https://mycareeratva.va.gov/CareerFitTool/

*yourself.* Ideally, you will blend all of these together into a healthy ratio. Consider the experience of the following employees:[6]

Sophia:

> *Like most employees, I learned new skills through on-the-job experiences. I identified and pursued experiences that allowed me to problem solve and take part in special assignments and other interesting day-to-day activities. These kinds of experiences include: Trying a new skill like making presentations, organizing activities, improving a process that is out of date, training others by demonstrating or explaining, and working on challenging tasks by trying to learn before seeking help.*

William:

> *I developed my skills by working with others and gaining insight into their knowledge and experience. Working with others involves meaningful relationships by gaining learning from feedback, observing role models, and networking. This includes finding formal and informal role models or mentors who are competent at a skill I want to learn, shadowing a high-performer I admire, informally soliciting feedback from my peers and manager, and having one-on-one discussions to work through problems.*

Mia:

> *I used formal training to advance my skills. Formal training classroom, workshop, or online training can occur in learning sessions like this one typically involves learning concepts first and then applying them to work-related activities. My formal training includes attending training courses, applying and participating in a formal leadership program, pursuing a degree and certificates in my areas of interest, and reading and studying from books and online resources.*

### Computers are the bicycle of your mind

As you work to train and develop your strengths, you will need to look for methods that can make you more efficient and effective in your strengths. And, over the long run, there is no better way to do so than to strategically employ new technology. The human body and mind, by themselves, are not nearly as powerful as that of wild animals in many ways, including primates. However, as Steve Jobs famously remarked (emphasis added):[7]

> I think one of the things that really separates us from the high primates is that we're tool builders. I read a study that measured the efficiency of locomotion for various species on the planet. The condor used the least energy to move a kilometer. Humans came in with a rather unimpressive showing about a third of the way down the list. It was not too proud of a showing for the crown of creation. That didn't look so good, but then someone at Scientific American had the insight to test the efficiency of locomotion for a man on a bicycle and a man on a bicycle blew the condor away. That's what a computer is to me: **the computer is the most remarkable tool that we've ever come up with. It's the equivalent of a bicycle for our minds.**

As Steve Jobs describes, the computer is the most powerful tool you can imagine for maximizing your strengths. Always be on the lookout for how new technology, especially computer technology, can improve your strengths and your work.[‡]

If you don't, there are consequences. Economists have found that workers who fail to adapt to new technology tend to lose out in the job market, and are at risk of facing reduced wages or even unemployment, due to a phenomenon known as "skill-biased technological change" (SBTC). SBTC theory holds that economic development today is largely driven by changes in technology that

---

[‡] I welcome you to listen to my weekly podcast, *CareerTech: Techniques and Technologies to Build Your Great Career*, available for free download via iTunes.

increasingly requires the employment of higher skilled workers. Workers who become more skilled in ways that work well with new technology have seen, and will see, increases in their wages and job opportunities; they are the ones moving up the socio-economic ladder. Meanwhile, workers who have not adapted to technological trends and who are not improving their skills are seeing their relative wages slide, and are more likely to end up unemployed.

Embrace the benefits that technology can have for your strengths and for your career. Technology is a strengths multiplier. With it – with this bicycle of the mind – you can soar further and faster than ever before.

### Don't worry, George, it's only a rough cut

> All of us who do creative work, we get into it because we have good taste. But there is this gap. For the first couple years you make stuff, it's just not that good. It's trying to be good, it has potential, but it's not. But your taste, the thing that got you into the game, is still killer. And your taste is why your work disappoints you. A lot of people never get past this phase, they quit. Most people I know who do interesting, creative work went through years of this.[8] – Ira Glass, host and producer of This American Life

Some time ago I became very interested in the art of film. I dabbled with aspirations to become a film critic, or even a screenwriter or director. DVDs had just become a thing and I was an early adopter of the technology. In their early stages DVDs were most known for two killer features they had over VHS cassettes: they didn't have to be rewound, and they had "extras." Those extras included features like audio commentary tracks with the creators of the film and special behind-the-scenes documentaries. I devoured the extras.

Soon after purchasing my first DVD player, I enrolled in a college film class and assigned myself the director Alfred

Hitchcock. Hitchcock was perhaps the most famous director of his generation, and, due to frequent cameos in his own films and his hosting a popular television show, probably the only director in the history of cinema whose physical visage was just as famous as the scenes in his films.

Of all of Hitchcock's many hits and classic films, "Psycho" is his most famous work. Released in black and white in 1960, it was not only by far the most profitable film of Hitchcock's career, it was also an aesthetic achievement. In 1992, it was officially deemed as such by the U.S. Library of Congress and was selected for preservation in the National Film Registry.

As a part of my college class assignment, I rented the special edition version of Psycho on DVD. Even four decades after its release, it held up very well; I loved it. It was clearly an original, very well made work of art. Eager to know more about its creation, I immediately began perusing the DVD extras. That's when I learned something that would stick with me for the rest of my life.

In one of the behind-the-scenes documentaries, editor George Tomasini reminisces about the difficulties they had in shooting the film and keeping the surprise ending a secret from not only the public, but also many members of the cast and film crew. Tomasini particularly remembers the moment when he and Hitchcock sat down to review the movie footage for the very first time. Tomasini could hardly contain his excitement. Even then, Hitchcock was famed for his directorial talent, and Psycho had the star-studded cast and high expectations accorded to films of his esteem. Tomasini's job as film editor was the opportunity of a lifetime, and he was about to be the first in the world to bear witness to Hitchcock's next great creation.

His excitement, however, did not last. Not long into the viewing, Tomasini began to feel uncomfortable. The footage was not what he had expected. And by the end of the viewing, he was *devastated*. The film, he thought, was *terrible*. All this time, money, the anticipation, it all would be for naught! He could not believe it.

As Tomasini sat there, aghast, Hitchcock could tell something was amiss with his editor. So he turned to Tomasini and said the words that would reassure him not only for the rest of the film's production, but for the rest of his career.

"Don't worry, George," Hitchcock reassured. "It's only a rough cut."

What surprised me most in this story is that Hitchcock didn't disagree with Tomasini. He *agreed* with him. He *knew* it was bad. But the elder Hitchcock saw something that the young Tomasini did not. Hitchcock knew the film *was supposed* to be bad – *it was only a rough cut.* Hitchcock saw the film's potential and the great work of art that it could (with a bit more work) still become.

Of course, Hitchcock and Tomasini then took that *terrible* cut of the movie and edited it into the version we know today.

And the rest, as they say, is history.

# CHAPTER 3

## Opportunity:

## What's in it for me?

*Creativity is just connecting things. When you ask creative people how they did something, they feel a little guilty because they didn't really do it, they just saw something. It seemed obvious to them after a while. – Steve Jobs*

## A brutal reality

The job market has been brutal since the 2008 recession, and if you're under the age of 30, it hasn't gotten much better since – despite overall reductions in the national unemployment rate. Young adult unemployment is at the highest sustained rate the country has seen since World War II[1] and more than 4 in 5 college seniors don't have jobs lined up after graduation.[2] And it gets worse – college is as expensive as ever, leaving the average graduate with nearly $30,000 in debt,[3] despite the fact that anywhere from one fourth to nearly half of employers don't think recent graduates are adequately prepared to be hired.[4] The situation is so bad that one-third of young adults have been forced to live with their parents.[5] So much for the American Dream.

It's not fun to have your dream shatter. But don't worry. If you follow my advice, yours won't.

## A crash course in labor economics

What if there are not enough jobs for everyone? You might be wondering. If so, how do you know that you can get a great job if there just aren't enough jobs out there? The answer is this: it is true that there are not enough *low skilled* jobs for everyone, at least not in the United States. Unlike some other countries, such as China or Brazil, the U.S. is too expensive to live in to sustain low skilled jobs on a large scale. But there continues to be no shortage of supply of high-skilled jobs in the U.S. The key is that you keep developing your skills in a way that matches the opportunities that are available. The more skilled you become, the more opportunities you will have, the more you will earn, and the higher degree of job security you will obtain.

In labor economics, there is a simple rule for how much you get paid: you get paid equal to what you produce. So if you produce $50,000 in value for a company, you will get paid that amount in wages (which, after company overhead and expenses, would actually equate to paying you closer to $25,000). If you want to be paid more, you need to produce more. There are exceptions, but generally speaking, if you want to earn more you either need to get better at your job or switch to a higher earning field.

In the Greatness Equation example I explained earlier, typically if you are a great employee you are making 16 widgets per year (to use an example), and if you are a good employee you are making 1 widget per year. Let's say each widget is worth $10,000. Let's also say you have a starting salary of $30,000 and that you start by being a good employee, so you're only producing 1 widget or $10,000 for your company. You are losing your company $20,000 (not including overhead). Your company however recognizes you are new and is willing to train you to see if you improve. You do improve – you follow the advice laid out in this book, you train and practice, and before you know it you're now a great employee producing 16 widgets worth $160,000. Think you'll be in line for a nice promotion? You bet you would be.

And that tends to be the case for most professions. Your organizations tend to lose money on you in the beginning. They're investing in you, hoping that you will learn and become a great employee. And if you don't, you will be gone, either terminated or you will likely quit on your own, and they will start the process all over again with someone else. But the fruit is there for the taking if you can align it with your Center, and if you put in the hours to get there.

There are, of course, exceptions to be aware of. There are two that I specifically want to speak about – first, the labor mobility exception, and second the shifting market exception.

Sometimes you may become that great employee producing 16 widgets to everyone else's 1 widget and may deserve the largest bonus and largest promotion, and still not get it. Many (outdated) organizations are still unfortunately not merit based and are based on outmoded concepts like seniority, or they use performance metrics that don't equate to what is actually valuable. In essence, they are playing a different game than you are. You're playing the right game (by producing the most value that you can) but your boss is playing something else. If that's the case, you may not get the promotion or bonus you deserve. However, the problem may be much worse than that. If your leadership doesn't understand how to produce value and how to incentivize it, then they are probably going to bankrupt your organization; not getting a promotion may be the least of your worries. *Now, you never know* – maybe they actually made the right call, maybe you weren't ready or a good fit for that promotion, or maybe you didn't actually deliver as much value as you think you did* – so don't make a hasty decision without thinking it through carefully. But if the organization is headed in the wrong direction and, as a result, not treating you appropriately, you need to be preparing for employment elsewhere.

But what if you can't find employment elsewhere? Unfortunately, despite what you may have read, it has actually become more difficult to switch jobs in the U.S. in recent decades, due to states' increasing licensing requirements that don't align with one another, and due to larger, more established businesses working with state and local governments to restrict the entry of newer businesses into their markets[6] and using abhorrent practices such as "non-compete" contract clauses that prevent employees

---

* Keep in mind that your value to your employer is not necessarily what you think it is. For example, if you made $160,000 in sales one year, your employer did not actually make $160,000 in value on those sales. They still have to pay overhead, including taxes, equipment, rent, and more, and have to also pay for the investment they are making in the other employees that produced much less than you did. In addition, the employer also has to pay for the risk that you will not produce $160,000 next year. Maybe you got lucky this year, and you will only produce $10,000 next year? Those are all factors that go into an employer's calculation of how much value you bring to your organization. Given how difficult this can be to calculate, employers will often determine your worth based on other factors, like how much it will cost to keep you (i.e. if you get a competing job offer from another company, your employer will usually match it or exceed it by a small amount). This is also why seniority-based systems are so appealing, it makes this calculation very easy for employers.

from seeking employment elsewhere.[7] Unless the U.S. federal or local governments intervene to relax these restrictions, the problem will remain for many individuals in the U.S. The best advice I can offer is to power through them as best you can – a lot of red tape isn't as scary as you think it is once you sit down and work through it. I think this rule goes for 80% of all red tape I have ever dealt with, so don't let it deter you and get you down.[†]

So what does all of this mean? The main consequence of a lack of labor mobility is a lack of negotiating power with your employer. So if you're producing $160,000 worth of value for your employer and they don't want to pay you what you're worth, but you have no where else to go, you don't have much of a choice but to accept their terms. At least until you find your next opportunity – which will come, if you *continue* to be great. Don't get discouraged, and never regress in the quality of your work, or you will guarantee you will never get that higher salary you deserve.

## Where jobs come from

In economics, jobs are created when a business estimates that if it hires one more person that person will, in turn, produce revenue equal to or greater than the cost of hiring that person. In essence: Will I make money by hiring another person or not? If the answer is yes, a job is created. If the answer is no, the job is not created.[‡]

The interesting part of this equation is *who* tends to be making the decision to create a new job the most. Contrary to popular belief, it's not large businesses, and it's not small businesses. It's

---

[†] If after powering through it you are still really having issues with red tape, consider getting a good lawyer. That's what they're there for. Your career is too important to let egomaniacal management hold you down. Fight back if you have to.

[‡] Since the typical employee stays with a job for about four or five years, employers will often estimate your future value over the next three-to-five years. (This varies of course; at one organization I surveyed the typical employee stayed with that organization for 11 years on average.)

not medium-sized businesses, either. It's *new* businesses. Economist Ron Jarmin has found that new businesses, which all start small but some will grow one day to be very large, are the only type of business that significantly create more jobs than they destroy.[8] The Kauffman Foundation released a similar study that found that start-ups accounted for all of the job growth in the U.S. that occurred from 1977 to 2005.[9] Large and small businesses that were not defined as new, meanwhile, actually produced *no new jobs* overall during the period studied.[§] As a result, this also means that a disproportionate amount of new *opportunities* (but by no means all!) will come from new businesses as well.

## What causes poverty

As you look to find a great job, you will probably be faced with one of two different kinds of salaries. Many people in the world work on a flat salary – you show up to work, say 9 a.m. to 5 p.m., and you get paid the same amount of money, no matter what. Others, like the self-employed, work on a revenue-based salary. If I sell a book, I earn some money, and I can use that money to eat tonight. If I don't, then I won't. Well, maybe it's not quite so stark for some of us, but for the poorest in the world this is the decision they often face, so you can imagine it is little wonder that many in the world, the poorest among us, are undernourished. The result is a sad, vicious one: a lack of nutrition, especially during pregnancy or early childhood, greatly stunts brain development, productivity, and your lifetime earnings – which means even less money to buy food.[10] (This is also true when it comes to other basic health items, such as vaccinations.) You would think, then, that given this positive relationship between buying more, nutritious food and earning more money, whenever the poorest had money left over,

---

[§] Unfortunately, since 2008 there have been fewer and fewer successful new businesses than ever (http://www.nytimes.com/2015/04/01/opinion/thomas-edsall-has-american-business-lost-its-mojo.html?emc=edit_ty_20150401&nl=opinion&nlid=34755528). This is the real source of weakness of the modern American economy. In the absence of improved government regulations to support new businesses, it's up to you to learn how to navigate these challenges to advance your career.

they would spend it on more, higher quality food. But they generally don't. A study in rural Indonesia found that men and women given iron supplements made the men able to work harder, which allowed them to earn more – they earned an additional $46 a year, in fact.[11] The cost of the iron supplement was only $7, so buying the iron was a no-brainer. But they didn't. So why didn't they? Why did they only take it when it was given for free? Other studies in Kenya and elsewhere have found similar effects.[12]

The answer appears to be in a study conducted in the Philippines.[13] A study there looked at employees who worked on one day on a flat salary and on others on a "piece rate," where the more the person worked, the more they got paid. That study found that the workers spent more money and ate better on days when they were working on a piece rate – the days when effort mattered. And that extra $46 in income in the Indonesian study? That was only for *self-employed* Indonesian workers; workers that took the iron supplements that were working on a flat wage saw no increase in income despite the fact that they were working better and working harder, and as a result they had no reason to pay the extra $7 to buy the iron and be more productive (and healthier and happier).

Ultimately, there are many reasons for poverty. For many, it's bad luck. For others, like the *self-employed* Indonesians who did not buy the $7 iron supplement even though it would make them $46 more, it was largely a lack of knowledge of how to invest in themselves. But one underappreciated reason that affects all of us, every day, is the terrible effect of poor incentives. If, like rural Indonesian workers, you are in an environment that does not care if you are healthy, happy and productive – or one that even *penalizes* it, by charging *you* for it and giving the benefit to someone else – what do you think will happen to you? You will in all likelihood be less healthy, less happy, and less productive.

Fortunately, there are always ways you can impact the environment around you so that it encourages you to be the best person you can be. Sometimes it means improving the physical space where you work, or looking at certain things differently, or negotiating a better work arrangement with your employer. Other times, it means planning an escape to a better work environment entirely. Keep all of these themes in mind as you read the rest of the book, particularly the chapters on passion, career planning, and leadership. They will have a large, yet underappreciated, impact on your career.

### Perseverance

*I'm convinced that about half of what separates successful entrepreneurs from the non-successful ones is pure perseverance. – Steve Jobs*

In the late 1960's Stanford psychologist Walter Mischel led a series of tests. In these tests Mischel famously placed a marshmallow in front of the child and presented him or her with a choice – you could have one marshmallow now, if you wanted. But if you declined, and *could* go fifteen minutes without eating it while it was sitting right in front of you, you would get two marshmallows instead. Predictably, some of the kids were able to last the fifteen minutes, while others did not.

Less predictable were the results the test would have many years later.

As it turned out, the results of this "marshmallow" test were incredibly predictive of the success the kids would have in their adult lives, much more so than any other factor, including their IQ.[14] Those kids who couldn't or wouldn't wait were more likely to have behavioral issues, poorer health, drug abuse, and lower SAT scores. Children who *did* wait the full fifteen minutes scored on average two hundred and ten points higher on their SAT's than those who waited only thirty seconds. The "delayers" went on to become successful professors, scientists, and politicians. The "rushers," meanwhile, were more likely to bounce from job to job.

Call it perseverance, call it delayed gratification – it is an extremely powerful force for your career success.

## How to get hired

Getting hired into a job is a lot like applying to college. You're judged on a mix of credentials, application materials, and the quality of competition you are up against. When you're applying to college, your credentials are your test scores and high school GPA. Your application is mostly your personal statement, and your competition depends largely on the prestige of the school you're applying for.

Getting hired works much the same way. Your credentials are your education and work experience. Your application is your resume and interview (or other assessment responses). And your competition depends on the labor market and the prestige of the position you're applying for – the relative supply and demand for that particular job.

Succeeding in getting hired depends largely on three factors: your *quality* as an applicant, your *timing* (or luck), and your persistence.

By persistence, I mostly mean the *quantity* of applications and networking activities that you do. Depending on the job market, be prepared to apply for one or two hundred jobs. There were times when I had to despite having very high credentials. It reminds me of a talk I heard by a well-known Latina author. After she wrote her first novel and was ready to submit it for publication, she sent it to more than 100 publishers. She heard back from just three of them. Of those three, only one included an offer to publish her novel. *But one was all it took.*

You need all three factors – quality, timing, and persistence – in your favor, and the more they are the better, but if just one of these three factors is off, you won't get hired into the job you want.

Sometimes the timing just doesn't work out – sometimes, like during a recession, companies just aren't hiring. And there is nothing you can do about it. Now, you can make up for a weakness in one area (such as bad timing) by improving the other two – you can apply to more positions (*persistence*) or you can improve your credentials and get better at interviewing or writing your resume (*quality*). But there are still minimum requirements you have to meet. The most perplexing for me is the credentials aspect, since an employer could always train its employees to learn new skills, but sadly very few employers like (or can afford) to train their employees, which means many would rather not hire anyone at all than hire someone who didn't already have experience doing the job they were hiring for. If you ever wondered why so many people want work but can't find it, this is why.

## The 100 Coffees Challenge

One nice trick to getting hired is that you can shortcut a good portion of the process through networking if you make a good enough impression on someone who is hiring. In Washington, DC I once roomed with an intern, Dan, who was struggling to find a full-time job despite his wide array of skills and credentials, which included a Master's degree. He had everything he needed to get hired into a good job, but the labor market was tough and he didn't know anyone in the area. He was sending in new job applications every day but getting nowhere. He was so discouraged he was ready to give up and move back to California. I thought he could solve his problem by focusing on networking, so I told him not to stop his DC job hunt until he had coffee with at least 100 new people. I made him a bet that if he did that – if he just had coffee with 100 new people – he would find a good job.

He took my advice, and dozens of coffees later Dan still hadn't found that job. It wasn't that he wasn't making a good impression on the people he was meeting with, he was, the *timing* was just off – the people he was meeting with weren't hiring. But to his credit, Dan kept trying, and at the end of each coffee he would ask for two names of people that he could meet with too. Using this referral method, by the time the number of coffees climbed into the 60's, Dan finally met someone *who knew someone* who was hiring. Since Dan had made so many good impressions on this person's other acquaintances, it wasn't long before he landed an interview and got hired for what turned out to be not just a good job, but a great one.

*The 100 Coffees Challenge*

❖ Set a goal to meet with 100 new people over coffee.

❖ At the end of each meeting, ask for the names of two additional people you should meet with.

❖ Don't ask outright for a job. Instead, ask for advice. Use your elevator pitch to explain who you are and what you have to offer. (Personally, my favorite question to ask is, "What is your secret to success?")

❖ Continue until you find the job you're looking for. Keep count of how many people you have met. Remain positive, and tell those who support you your running tally to keep the positivity going: "Off to have my 25th coffee today!" "Today is lucky coffee number 52!"

Remember, you don't need to start off with your dream job – you can always find a good enough one that is close to it, and then work on getting promoted into it.

### Recruitment: Will you work for me?

I have spent a good portion of my career recruiting employees and interns for other managers, as well as recruiting new employees and interns to work for me. In my opinion, hiring and integrating a new employee is the single most important, and most complex, action a manager will ever take. You get it right, and your team can reap the benefits for years, if not decades. If you get it wrong, you expose your team to not only a potential negative influence, but, if the employee is particularly irresponsible, you may find yourself on the wrong end of a lawsuit or investigation, and the possible end of your career.

Hiring a new employee is a very high-stakes affair.

Just think about that for a moment when you are applying for a new job. Just imagine the risk that the hiring manager would be taking on by hiring you. And also imagine all the effort that went into even giving you that interview. In many organizations, and particularly in government jobs, the hiring process can be a very lengthy and challenging process. It takes a certain amount of dedication to even create the job opening to begin with. You should maintain a healthy amount of respect for the people who created that opening for you.

But many applicants don't. They treat a new potential job – whether it's in the application phase, or after being hired – as if it's an entitlement. They don't show appreciation for the immense effort that it took to bring them there, or for the risk that the organization is taking on by hiring them or considering to, and for the great amount of trust that the hiring manager will have placed in them. Employees with this mindset are often the first to complain, the first to leave the office, the first to get discouraged, and the last to say thank you. Not only do they not add value to the organization, they tend to subtract it – meaning it would've been better if the organization had hired no one rather than hire them.

This is what is going through the mind of every hiring manager when she reviews your application. Keep that in mind, and at every opportunity show that you understand where she is coming from and that, if you're hired, you're not going to be one of "those" employees.

## How to get promoted

If you want to get promoted, you can focus on doing two things – doing great work, and creating successful projects. (Though you shouldn't stop there – be sure to also read the sections on networking and successfully navigating office politics.)

Doing great work, like having a great career, is a function of the Center described earlier – playing to your strengths, passion, and the opportunities in front of you. You really need all three to be great at even relatively small projects.

As described in the chapter on passion, which also covers issues related to workplace satisfaction, in his book *Outliers: The Story of Success*, Malcolm Gladwell wrote that for work to be satisfying it must have three qualities: "autonomy, complexity, and a connection between effort and reward." Think of opportunities in that way. Where can I do work that I can have a degree of freedom over how I conduct my work (*autonomy*), where the job is relatively challenging for me (*complexity*), and I will be *rewarded* for my efforts?

In many instances, injecting these qualities into your work is as simple as changing your perception. I find a natural tendency for many people to follow orders literally, and to do the minimum required, if for no other reason than to get you what you want as soon as possible and to move on to the next assignment. This is not necessarily a bad thing, but too much of it can reduce your sense of autonomy and the complexity of the assignment. Whenever you're given a mundane task, think about how you can make it more complex. Whenever you're being micromanaged, think about working on a task that will fly under the radar and give you more freedom. And always, always have a keen eye for whatever you know has a reward involved – and see if you can align your work to obtain it.

The best way to do this is to create a project.

### Creating projects

The good news is there is an easy way to meet all three of these qualities in nearly every work place – start a new project. It also happens to be an essential element of getting your next promotion. It is by far the best thing you can do with whatever spare time you may have at the office. You can kill two birds with one stone – make yourself happier and advance your career all at the same time.

To start, just follow these five steps:

1. Imagine making something cool. Really cool. A website, training materials, a big speech, a video, presentation, or computer program. Or simply a new process. It doesn't matter, just imagine it.

2. Finish your non-cool tasks for the day quickly, but do them well – it is your job, after all. Do them as efficiently as possible so that you have plenty of time left in the day to...

3. ...Mentally sketch out your plan to build your really cool thing. As you begin developing your really cool idea, which can (and maybe should) include iterations of research, sketches, models, and samples, constantly ask yourself this question: "How can I make this help my boss?" (If you're still in school, ask yourself how can you get school credit or school funding for it.) Tweak your original idea over and over again until you've reached the point where you have no doubt that you have a really cool idea that will definitely help your boss. Bounce the idea off of other employees and mentors to further refine it if you can. This could take more than one day, but that's ok.

The easiest way to do this is to connect it to a strategic goal that your boss is tasked with achieving. If you can, you will score easy points. Also, be sure to design your idea in a way that meets the needs of as many relevant stakeholders or clients as you can without losing its quality.

4. Present the idea to your boss. This can be as simple as a 30-second elevator pitch, or as complex as a formal 30-minute presentation. It's a skill that you may need more practice with. You can find help with this in the chapter on interviewing. In any event, be sure to practice on your own as much as possible first. If all goes well, go to step 5.

5. Celebrate. (And then get to work.)

*Stay hungry. Stay foolish. – Steve Jobs*

Remember, most ideas fail, and, in my research at least, nearly every successful idea in history originated from a failed one. If your idea doesn't work, don't worry! Come up with another one and repeat steps 1-4. As long as you are learning and getting better, you will start to see your ideas become successes. Not only have I gotten many ideas off the ground this way, even failed ideas of mine have had a way of coming back to life later. As a professor of mine once said, sometimes it takes time for new ideas to sink in. Don't ever put all of your eggs into one idea basket, but don't give up on your great idea the first time it gets shut down either – keep it in your back pocket and see if it sinks in later. It just might.

*People think focus means saying yes to things you've got to focus on. But that's not what it means at all. It means saying no to the hundred good ideas that there are. You have to pick carefully.*

*Innovation is saying no to a thousand things. That's true for companies, and it's true for products.... We're always thinking about new markets we could enter, but it's only by saying no that you can concentrate on the things that are really important. – Steve Jobs*

### Finding blue oceans

In 2005, the video game company known as Nintendo was drowning. At that point, Sony's PlayStation 2 had demolished Nintendo's latest console, the GameCube, in head-to-head sales, and by the end of the year Microsoft had released the popular Xbox 360. Nintendo, which had been losing market share for a full decade by this point, was now a distant third in the cutting edge console race.

But then something changed – Nintendo gave up. It gave up the technology wars. Or to be more precise, it gave up the *graphics* technology wars. Nintendo had lost the competition to deliver the fastest processors with the most technical power to consumer electronics giant Sony and global software powerhouse Microsoft, who were more than happy to sell their advanced console hardware at a loss so they could compete with Nintendo's weaker and cheaper consoles, in order to make their profits from selling video game licenses to developers. Nintendo refused to adopt this strategy and paid dearly for it.

Until they gave up.

Instead of slogging in third place, Nintendo found a shortcut. Nintendo adopted a strategy known as Blue Ocean Strategy. That theory defined the business world as having both red oceans and blue oceans. In the red oceans, competition was fierce, rules were very defined, the profit margins were small, and the stakes were very high. The red ocean represents the blood in the water that results from this fierce battle. In blue oceans meanwhile, which were simply undiscovered markets, the game was wide open to be defined, and the possibilities – and profits – were, in a sense, endless.

When Nintendo introduced the Wii to compete with the Xbox 360 and PlayStation 3 it was panned by critics for its graphic inferiority. But it was a smashing success and handily outsold both of its competitors. The reason was because it found a blue ocean.

It reached a new market – people who enjoyed games, but didn't enjoy the complexity and violence that had made the Xbox and PlayStation famous. The Wii offered them an alternative with its simple motion-controlled games and exercises.

### Fame from a blog comment

In order to create those projects that will advance your career and help you get those promotions, you need to find your own blue oceans. In your office, it might be creating new training or employing new technology. One great blue ocean that I discovered in my first career was internships. While permanent employees were a definite red ocean with many cumbersome regulations and policies, internships and interns were the opposite. So whenever I had a new innovative idea that I thought would benefit our workforce, I started by testing it with the organization's hundreds of interns – a blue ocean. Consider also the example of 26-year-old graduate student Matthew Rognlie who recently gained fame in his field of economics via a simple blog comment post – not an actual blog *post*, he simply posted a thoughtful *comment* on another person's blog – critiquing the theories of one of the world's most influential economic thinkers.[15] Rognlie's insightful blog *comment* was picked up by academics and media; since then he has gone on to publish an influential paper on the subject and has been cited by the preeminent publication *The Economist*. Rognlie didn't need any special access to post that blog comment, he just needed to use that opportunity wisely, and he did. And now, Rognlie has probably set himself up for success for the rest of his life – what employer is not going to want to hire *him*?

### Projects 101

Allow me to be blunt – you will never achieve anything great without creating a project of some sort. Go ahead and try and think of an example, because I can't.

Now that I've sold you on taking project management seriously, let's brush up on project management training. The essence of project management can be boiled down to one simple concept, known as the Project Management Triangle or the "Iron Triangle":

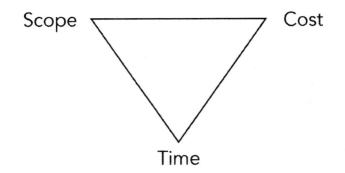

Scope is the size of your project, the cost could be financial or any other resource you have to spend (like your own personal stress), and time is essentially how fast you can complete the project. The triangle represents the constant trade offs you have to make between speed, size, and cost to complete your project successfully.

Here is the key: *unless you want a failed project, you only get to prioritize two of these. You must be flexible on at least one factor at any given time.* For example, you cannot create a project that is simultaneously cheap, fast, and large. It will fail. Instead, you must choose. To help you understand, here are three examples for you to choose from. You can choose only one of the following approaches at any given time:

First, you could create:

1) *A project that is cheap and fast but small.* For example, you could volunteer to deliver a low-tech presentation to a group of 10 people, with no visual aids and with just one day to prepare.

Great! That project was a smash hit. Now let's say that goes so well you want to make it bigger. If so, alternatively you could choose:

2) *A project that is cheap and large but slow.* Instead of a small but quick presentation, this would instead be a do-it-yourself zero budget lecture to 200 people with visual aids and handouts – that also takes you months to prepare.

Amazing! You're two for two. Finally, imagine the CEO of your company is in town on a whim, and your next huge presentation just got moved up to *tomorrow.* There is *no way* you yourself can create all of the materials in time to do it tomorrow, but the show must go on, and it must be perfect! So what do you do to make sure it's still a success? You could choose:

3) *A project that is fast and large but expensive.* You break out the company credit card and call in a professional – at double their normal rate, due to the short notice – to fill in and deliver the large, high-tech lecture quickly and flawlessly – and on just one day's notice.

It's up to you to determine when, where, and why to use which one of these three project versions.

The most important criteria you should use when determining which of the three project versions to use should be your Center. Is a project dead center within your Center? Then you should consider #1 or #2 and volunteering to do it for cheap or even for free to build your skills in it, even if it takes you many months (or years) to learn and do it properly. (If you can get financial support to do it great, feel free to go for #3).

Now what if the project is outside of your Center and you still must figure out a plan to complete it? That is a great candidate for category number three – pay the money to hire a professional to do it the right way. And if you have time to plan this project well in advance, do so, you can get a much better rate and save your project quite a bit of money by booking in advance. Just like hiring someone to do your taxes or your dry cleaning, if it's really not in your interest to do it yourself then hire the right person to do it and forget about it.

I use all three styles of project management on a near daily basis in the many projects I manage, and to great effect. Once you get the hang of it, you can (and should) too.

### Failing is good – if you fail small

In his book *Little Bets: How Breakthrough Ideas Emerge from Small Discoveries*, Peter Sims documents how the best professionals and companies cultivate a culture of using failure to succeed. He begins with famous comedian Chris Rock.[16]

Before performing his large, national comedic routines, Chris Rock performs as many as forty to fifty times in small venues near his home, often showing up unannounced. Most of his jokes perform terribly. But a few go over really well, including some that Rock never would have guessed. He ends up going through hundreds of jokes just find a few that will make it into his larger routine. The satirical newspaper *The Onion* is similar, publishing only about three percent of the headlines its writers think up.

As Sims writes, this approach is hardly unique to Chris Rock and *The Onion*. It's been used to astonishing success throughout the business world, including by Apple, prize-winning architect Frank Gehry, and Pixar. I use this approach almost every day, and you should try to as well.

The Sims *Little Bets* approach is as follows:[17]

- ❖ *Experiment.* As Sims explains, "Learn by doing. Fail quickly to learn fast. Develop experiments and prototypes to gather insights, identify problems, and build up to creative ideas, like Beethoven did in order to discover new musical styles and forms."

- ❖ *Play.* Enjoy yourself! Create an environment where you can have fun. Use music and images of kittens if it helps.

- ❖ *Immerse.* Get into the world. Walk around, meet people, call them up. Put yourself in someone else's shoes.

- ❖ *Define.* Sims writes, "Use insights gathered throughout the process to define specific problems and needs before solving them, just as the Google founders did when they realized that their library search algorithm could address a much larger problem."

- ❖ *Reorient.* Sims: "Be flexible in pursuit of larger goals and aspirations, making good use of small wins to make necessary pivots and chart the course to completion."

- ❖ *Iterate.* Sims: "Repeat, refine, and test frequently armed with better insights, information, and assumptions as time goes on, as Chris rock does to perfect his act."

**Don't just sit and think about doing something great, try to do it now.** See how it goes and learn from it. I can't tell you how many aspiring writers I've given the following advice to: If you want to be a writer, then write. Writers write. Non-writers don't. Singers sing, speakers speak, leaders lead.

# [Do]'ers [do].

## Win all the awards

Well, you can't win them all, but you can win your fair share. Consider how important winning awards and accolades are for getting your next job or promotion. If you follow the steps above, you will have many opportunities to win awards. But make sure to work backwards if you can – think of what the award or accolade requires for you to win it, then see if you can plan your project around winning that award. Awards add up and can not only be a great motivator but an important line on your resume.

## Office politics

Navigating office politics is crucial to your success – even if you don't work in an office! People need each other to build great things. You will always need something from someone else to succeed – skills, time, funds, training, a job, a promotion, a staff person or team-member. More than ever given the prevalence of the internet and social networking, your relationships with others will go a long way in determining your ultimate success.

Office politics can be fickle and treacherous, so never assume you have it mastered. All it takes is one ugly incident to grind your beloved project, and potentially your career, to a halt.

On the other hand, don't be afraid either. Embrace the human element. If you can understand why others do what they do, you can bring them into your team and transform your small successes into much larger ones. Winning in office politics can start with something as simple as cleaning out the office coffee pot.[18]

## Maslow's Hierarchy of Needs

The key to understanding what motivates others was first developed by social psychologist Abraham Maslow. He described a hierarchy of needs that every individual has:

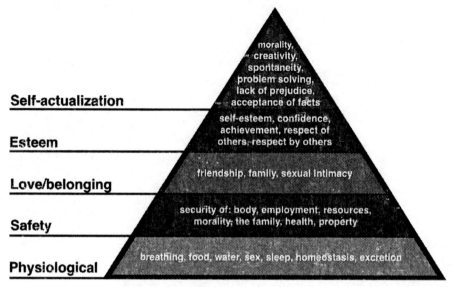

**Self-actualization** — morality, creativity, spontaneity, problem solving, lack of prejudice, acceptance of facts

**Esteem** — self-esteem, confidence, achievement, respect of others, respect by others

**Love/belonging** — friendship, family, sexual intimacy

**Safety** — security of: body, employment, resources, morality, the family, health, property

**Physiological** — breathing, food, water, sex, sleep, homeostasis, excretion

*Maslow's Hierarchy of Needs*[19]

The needs at the bottom are the first, but not necessarily the most powerful – it depends on the person's situation. For example, a woman who is starving probably doesn't worry too much about issues like bias in the media, for example; she has more pressing physiological needs. However, if she were living a comfortable middle class life, she probably isn't as motivated by the prospect of a free lunch as she would be if she were homeless. In this instance, you should probably appeal to a higher need, like esteem or my favorite, self-actualization.

Self-actualization means reaching your Center – merging your desire to be the you that you want to be with the opportunities and strengths you have. If you appeal to that, people will respond very well to it as well.

Navigating office politics means understanding why other people behave the way they do. Use Maslow's hierarchy to understand their motivations – then use it to your advantage to help you accomplish your goals and advance your projects.

## Trust

*Contrary to what most people believe, trust is not some soft, illusive quality that you either have or you don't; rather trust is a pragmatic, tangible, actionable asset that you can create.*[20] – Stephen M.R. Covey

Has there ever been anyone you refused to work with? Or that you avoided working with? Think of why that was. I would bet that you did not trust that person. The converse is true too – there are people that, at one point, probably avoided you too, for the same reason.

Trust, as Stephen M.R. Covey writes in his book *The Speed of Trust: The One Thing That Changes Everything*, truly does change everything. You could try anything in your career, but if people don't trust you, what can you possibly accomplish? Everything in your life can speed up if you have a bit more trust. You will gain more autonomy, more responsibility, more flexibility. And, as a result, more opportunities.

The good news is that trust is actually very easy to build with simple behaviors. Be sure to incorporate Covey's thirteen behaviors he provides to make sure you are building the trust you need to be successful:[21]

- ❖ Talk Straight.
- ❖ Demonstrate Respect.
- ❖ Create Transparency.
- ❖ Right Wrongs.
- ❖ Show Loyalty.
- ❖ Deliver Results.
- ❖ Get Better.
- ❖ Confront Reality.

❖   Clarify Expectations.

❖   Practice Accountability.

❖   Listen First.

❖   Keep Commitments.

❖   Extend Trust.

## Tips for creating better work relationships

Good work relationships are critical for success and unlocking opportunities for you. I don't think I could have accomplished anything of substance if I didn't have that going for me. My strategy for that is pretty simple, so I thought I'd share.

*Go at their pace.* If your coworker wants coffee, have coffee. If they prefer happy hour, go to happy hour. If you don't know, suggest what works for you. But if they don't like it, don't take it personally, and see if you can come up with another approach that works for both of you.

Meet them where they are, not where you want them to be. If your coworker is not a social person, don't get upset if they don't want to go to a group outing. If they are having a bad day, don't talk to them the same way as if they were having a good day. Pay close attention to who they are and how they are feeling, and then adjust your approach accordingly.

Give them what they need. An easy way to get on my bad side is to not do what I need from you. So if someone asks you for something, and you agree to do it, do it and do it quickly. If this is hard for you, then either get better at it, or don't agree to do it in the first place.

## How to work with people you dislike

Sometimes, you just don't *want* to work with that person, no matter what they may offer you. There are two easy, but not very good, solutions for working with people you dislike: Don't work with them, by either excluding them from your team or finding another project or another job. The second poor solution is to limit your relationship with that person. Focus exclusively on the work you do together and be cautious in your communication to make sure your dislike does not show and that your work still gets done.

But there is a much better option than those two, which is to *find something that you like about the person*. In other words, just stop disliking them. Why bother? I've worked with *thousands* of people and I can hardly think of anyone that I actively dislike. It's almost impossible for me to not be able to find something that I like about a person. Once I do, I focus on that, and life becomes so much easier. You should try doing the same.

If you think that you need to agree with someone on everything or even most things in life before you can like them, you're setting yourself up for a very disappointing life.

### Forgiveness

Related to this point is the power of forgiveness and the apology. I forgive everyone that is sorry for the mistake they made. Why not? Why don't you? What do you possibly have to gain by not forgiving? What logical or theological reason could you have for not forgiving someone for something they are genuinely sorry for? Related to *that*, if *you* are guilty of a mistake, apologize early and often. Trust me, it's important. People remember if you do or don't apologize for your mistakes.

Stanford University has a very interesting initiative called the Stanford Forgiveness Projects, which as of 2010 was headed by Dr. Frederic Luskin. According to Dr. Luskin, "Forgiveness has been shown to reduce anger, hurt, depression and stress and lead to greater feelings of optimism, hope, compassion and self confidence." Those who know me well know that I am an evangelist for forgiveness. My personal belief in forgiveness goes back to my Catholic upbringing, but I think it's extremely important for all walks of life, including the workplace.

On his website, Dr. Luskin includes the results of a corporate pilot his organization conducted, which taught techniques for forgiveness as a part of a series of interpersonal workshops:[22]

> *Results showed gross dealer concession (sales) increased for the first group of advisors an average of 18%, for the second group of advisors an average increase of 24%, for the third group an average of 24%, for the fourth group of advisors an average of 46%, for the fifth group an average of 25% for the sixth group an average increase of 14% and for the seventh group 30%.*

Quality of life, anger and physical vitality measures also demonstrated statistically significant beginning to end positive change. Forgiveness is powerful. If you're interested in learning more, PsychologyTools.org has tools and materials on its website.

The next time someone does something that upsets you, it also helps to remember Hanlon's razor – Never attribute to malice what can be adequately explained by incompetence.[23] And if it does turn out to be malice, consider preacher Joel Osteen's advice: "When we forgive others, we take away their power to hurt us."[24]

### The bottom line

As you go forth and think about new opportunities, you will have to think about your bottom line. You'll find that you'll inevitably be faced with the wrong kinds. In the federal government, for example, bottom lines are all too often the wrong things. I often spent far more time measuring things like how many conferences we did than how many of our employees had the training they needed to succeed. Which one do you think is actually more important to greatness? Counting how many meetings we have, or making sure our employees actually know what they're doing on the job?

On the individual level, the opportunity circle means finding what opportunities are around you that can lead to greatness –

Does your office have a bottom line that you can achieve? That you can be great at? Does it have opportunities in the way of funding or staff that you can use to fill this critical need? Are there projects you can propose that you can do to meet these needs given the resources you have? Are there people, places, or items that aren't getting the attention that they need that you can do something about? Think broadly.

On the organizational level, it means making sure that your organization, or team, is focusing on those bottom lines that can lead your organization to greatness. It's very easy to fall into the trap of measuring what everyone else tells you to measure, or what is easy to measure, and striving to be great at that, when the opportunity just isn't there. The result will only be just "good enough," or worse.

### What opportunity looks like

Consider the examples of the following employees:[25]

Daniel:

> I am an engaged employee because I am proactive – I take action when I see a problem. I voluntarily get involved in finding a solution rather than waiting to ask my supervisor or coworkers for help. By finding opportunities to help, I advance my career development and learn new, valuable skills.

Isabella:

> I feel most engaged when I go the extra mile, engaging in behavior sometimes called "discretionary effort." Giving discretionary effort means that you perform at a higher level than is expected of you, like giving higher quality customer service by checking in with your customers even when you aren't asked to do so. Using the career development tools available online, I found my interest in helping others and am now much more engaged in my work.

Alex:

> I am flexible and adapt well to change. Even if your work tasks rarely veer from the norm, at some point your work conditions will likely change. Being flexible and adaptable ensures these changes will not disrupt your work, and that you will continue to feel engaged in your job.

Chloe:

> I am willing to take on unexpected responsibilities, viewing them as opportunities for skill development. Rather than responding to these extra tasks by saying, "that's not my job," I seem them as growth opportunities that can help me advance in my career path, and I also know that supporting my colleagues helps form positive connections between us.

# CHAPTER 4

## *Passion:* Who am I?

*I am an American soldier.*

*I am a Warrior and a member of a team.*

*I serve the people of the United States, and live the Army Values.*

*I will always place the mission first.*

*I will never accept defeat.*

*I will never quit.*

*I will never leave a fallen comrade.*

*I am disciplined, physically and mentally tough, trained and proficient in my warrior tasks and drills.*

*I always maintain my arms, my equipment, and myself. I am an expert and I am a professional.*

*I stand ready to deploy, engage, and destroy the enemies of the United States of America in close combat.*

*I am a guardian of freedom and the American way of life.*

*I am an American Soldier.*[1] *– The Soldier's Creed*

In her book, *It's Your Career: OWN IT!*, career development expert Alice Muellerweiss provides a method to help you understand your passion. She has you ask yourself: *Who am I? What do I value? What are my interests?* Think of these as you read this chapter (I suggest reading her book in full as well). For Alice, a large part of her character and values were formed when she first joined the U.S. Army, where she was taught the Soldier's Creed, above, which helps provide answers to these questions for its soldiers. As an exercise try thinking of your own creed as well.

You will probably find that your values are different than the Soldier's Creed. That's ok, everyone values different things in life for a good reason; it helps us each focus our limited attention and resources. One of the secrets to greatness is what you choose to devote your limited attention to. A certain portion of that is not in your control – they are responsibilities, like taking out the trash or filing a report, that you simply must do. But others are in your control, like how you express a passion for design or the written language. It is up to you to fill as much discretionary time as you can for those passions that you care most about.

You should think about your passions broadly, as it will open up new opportunities for you as well. If you truly are passionate for example about interior design, could you not also become passionate about projects for office renovation, or new facilities? If you truly are passionate about the written language, could you not also become passionate about the report that you must file anyway, which also happens to express the written language that you care so much about? If you truly are passionate about meeting new people, couldn't you also volunteer to greet new customers?

In a sense, understanding passion is as much about discovery as it is about perception. One man's trash is another man's treasure, and sometimes one person's trash can be her own treasure – she just doesn't know it yet.

If the value of something to you is so obvious that you can't understand why people ask you about it, that it causes people to have a bewildered look on their face when you try to describe it to them, you know you've found a passion.

If you're still having trouble with this please take the MyCareer@VA Career Fit Tool. It will display career fields that it thinks you may be passionate about. This can give you ideas not only for different careers, but also different projects that you can bring into your current job. If it says for example being an Attorney might be a good fit for you, consider taking on legal work within your current job, such as working on contracts. You may discover a new passion that can help you advance your career.

### The happiness advantage

Shawn Anchor writes in his book *The Happiness Advantage* that if you write three things that you are grateful for on a piece of paper every morning at work, you will outperform your colleagues that don't.[*] The reason why is that expressing gratitude makes you happier, and happiness leads to better work. We often have it backwards – we think that more success will lead us to more happiness. But for your brain, success is never enough – once you obtain a goal, your mind just moves the goalposts even further. Success becomes akin to an addiction – you get more, so you need more. By focusing on what makes you happy now, by doing something as simple as writing three things you are grateful for on a piece of paper, you will be more successful right now.

A side benefit to this habit of expressing gratitude is that you can also start to better notice what it is that you are truly passionate about. There are some things you will notice that you will never be very grateful for, because the truth of the matter is, you just are not very passionate about them – they are unimportant to you.

---

[*] All things being equal.

## Optimism leads to success

Imagine you are fighting a friendly rebellion led by young relatives, a rag-tag bunch of scurrilous minions, aged 8 to 10 years old. While rough housing with the young ones an errant elbow happens to hit one of the children. Oncoming tears mean the arrival of the child's mother and an end to the war games. Action is needed, so you say "Hey there," attempting to head off the tears before they flow. "Look how tough you are! You're the toughest fighter ever! You're *the Wolverine!*"

Those two words yield the smile they so desperately seek, and the rebel child leaps back into action, healed by his newfound mutant powers. His fists extend and the war games resume!

Shawn Anchor, author of *The Happiness Advantage*, tells a similar story of how he stopped his little sister from crying by pretending she was a unicorn with magical powers.[2] Anchor's story is an introduction to a much larger idea: the relationship between optimism and success.

According to Good Think, Anchor's company, optimism of the kind that resuscitated the rebel child above has an extremely high correlation with job-related success. 75% of job-related successes in fact, a Good Think study found, can be predicted by optimism levels, social support, and the ability to see stress as a challenge instead of a threat. IQ, meanwhile, has a disastrous correlation of just 25%.[3]

The reason why appears to be biological. A sense of happiness releases dopamine in the brain. Dopamine then increases the brain's ability to learn. And learning leads to success.

No wonder, then, that history is littered with successful leaders who were known more by their unyielding optimism – Ronald Reagan, Bill Clinton – than their academic credentials. Optimism, and the ability to see challenges as obstacles to be overcome and not dispiriting threats, may be what leaders need most to lead. You certainly need it to be passionate, and as a result, to be great.

Optimism however is not as simple as it seems. It can easily be associated with foolishness and naiveté, and if others take it as such, you will not be taken seriously. You have to ground your optimism in an underlying truth – the truth that you are happy with what you are doing, the way that you are doing it, and are confidant that good results will come of it.

## Enhancing your passion

In any given moment there may be many tiny obstacles between you and your passion, like snow blocking a driveway. Removing this debris can be at times incredibly easy to forget, we often watch as it builds up higher and higher and higher. It requires quite a bit of discipline and foresight to do well consistently. But the results can be grand.

How many times have you stubbed your toe? Forgot your keys? Failed to charge your phone? Read a hostile email? Sent a hostile email by chance?

Do you recall accomplishing anything great that day after that occurred? You may have, but chances are you were not as great as you could have been that day after that initial negativity. This negative debris probably led to a negative attitude that slowed you down, if not derailed you entirely.

Tom Rath and Donald Clifton's *How Full Is Your Bucket* documents this principle at work in the fields of business, management and personal relationships over a 40-year span. Rath and Clifton explain that we all have "buckets" that must be filled with positive psychology for us to be productive. Something good happens – you sip that fresh cup of coffee; your favorite blend – and your bucket fills up a bit. Something bad happens – you spill that coffee on your lap, ouch – and your bucket draws down. The beautiful thing about this concept is that, with a little foresight, you can exercise a great deal of control over your own personal "bucket," and make sure that you fill your bucket as much as possible every day, and the buckets of others – who will then in turn fill your bucket with more gratitude, praise, and recognition as well.

In China, this concept is well ensconced within Feng Shui. Instead of a "bucket," Feng Shui holds that we all have energy, which in Chinese is called "chi." This energy is not only within you, it permeates everything around you. The main goal of Feng Shui is to attract, direct, and nourish the "flow" of energy inside your home so as to better support the energy that is inside of you. You can and should apply this concept to your office environment as well.

In concrete terms, think of the jagged edges or clutter around your home that might cut into your knee, shin, or toe as you walk around. When your home or office inflicts this kind of pain on you, what do you think happens to your energy? It goes down, but it's even worse than you think. Not only does your body feel immediate pain and distraction, you also lose a degree of subconscious trust and comfort in the area itself, which continues to harm your energy, again and again, even if you never stub your toe again. That warm feeling that we all want to get as we enter our home or office is dependent on what happens to us inside of our home or office, and how it is physically designed to treat us.

Think of your health. Every ounce of healthy food that you put into your body, those ever green vegetables, and every bit of exercise that you do adds up to more or less comprise your overall health. We know this. It's the same concept as the bucket or Feng Shui, and it applies to your career in the same way. How often have you accomplished anything great while you were sick? How often did your colleagues accomplish anything great while they were sick?

I know what you're thinking: Hardly ever, and likely never. These seemingly trivial examples are just a few of the myriad ways you can lose your passion, and, as a result, your greatness.

Ultimately, it is critical to understand what your passion is and what it is not. It is a discovery and it is a deliberate process. It is not an order, it is not a decision. You cannot merely decide to become passionate about something, nor order others to become passionate about it. You may discover, after careful examination and research, that you are actually passionate about something that you were not fully aware of, or that you may have actually looked down upon for social reasons – that you may, after thinking it over a bit, be passionate about that report you are tasked to write after all, once you realized that it's actually an opportunity for you to express your passion for something you are good at – such as writing, or numbers, or the truth – when, initially, you were reluctant. After discovering your true, un-socially distorted passions, you can then enhance them by spending more time on the parts you love, and by cleaning up all of that negative debris that is around you that is little by little wasting your time.

### When in doubt, kittens

Don't underestimate the little things that can enhance your passion – like kittens. Hiroshima University ran a number of experiments and found that people who looked at pictures of puppies or kittens subsequently had higher levels of concentration on their work.[4]

Music can also be a powerful way to boost your mood and productivity. U.K. music licensing organizations commissioned a survey that found that 77 percent of businesses surveyed said that playing music in the workplace increased staff morale and improved the atmosphere.[5]

### Job satisfaction

In his book *Outliers: The Story of Success*, Malcolm Gladwell wrote that for work to be satisfying it must have three qualities: "autonomy, complexity, and a connection between effort and reward." You could consider these elements to be the chemistry behind work optimism.

You can find greater autonomy by searching for Blue Oceans as described in the chapter on opportunity.

You can find greater complexity in your work by changing your sense of perspective and appreciation of the nature of your work.

*WANTED: JOB OPENING*

*DESCRIPTION: Clicks keys on the keyboard. Sits in on long meetings. Receives daily criticism and responds to it on behalf of the organization.*

*TITLE: President of the United States.*

Complexity can be added into every work assignment in a fulfilling way if you think about it – whether by increasing its design; content; electronic automation; or exposure (marketing). Nearly all work is important if done well and can benefit someone. Apple, the world's most profitable company, is famous for its deeply embedded culture of appreciation for different disciplines across the sciences and the liberal arts. An appreciation of the complexity that is required to make effective tools and services is inspirational in of itself, and instills with it a desire to learn more about the assignment, and to achieve more in accomplishing it.

Apple was built on Steve Jobs's unyielding dedication to design and craftsmanship. Steve Jobs consistently traced this passion to his father, a carpenter, who would dedicate equal amounts of exacting effort to the back panels of his cabinets, even though it was meaningless because that part was hidden from view. After the Macintosh was released, Jobs stated:[6]

> *When you're a carpenter making a beautiful chest of drawers, you're not going to use a piece of plywood on the back, even though it faces the wall and nobody will ever see it. You'll know it's there, so you're going to use a beautiful piece of wood in the*

*back. For you to sleep well at night, the aesthetic, the quality,*
*has to be carried all the way through.*

As stated earlier, the final part of Gladwell's work-happiness formula is the connection between effort and reward. The first instinct for many of us is to think of monetary rewards, though money can be one of the weakest human motivators. Dr. Abraham Maslow, a 20th-century pioneer of developmental psychology, wrote that human beings have a hierarchy of needs, of which physiological needs like food and shelter – and the money that buys them –are the first, but only the most basic. If these needs are being met, they cease to be as powerful as the other needs that Maslow cites, at the top of which is *self-actualization*. Self-actualization is where morality and creativity are found. Between self-actualization, the top of the pyramid, and physiological needs, the bottom, are other more common forms of reward: esteem, and love or belonging.

Money is the lowest motivator, love is in the middle, and being *the you that you want to be*? That is the highest.

When connecting effort to reward, it's important to reach to the top of Maslow's pyramid. Beyond monetary reward, belonging and esteem are important, but even beyond that, the moral component is truly the highest. This is what motivates mankind above all, and what creates the happiness with work that leads to success.

Remember: self-actualization in of itself does not have to be complex. It can be a simple motivational YouTube video.

### The Paradox of Choice

You would think that having more choices makes you happier. Turns out, that's not true at all. As Barry Schwartz explains in his book and accompanying Ted Talk, *The Paradox of Choice: Why More Is Less*, too many choices will make you unhappy.[7] This is why you tend to get less done when you have *all day* to get your errands done, as opposed to having only one or two hours. Or why you may find it refreshing to not be around your smart phone. Or why you enjoy having someone else plan a trip for you. Or why you make better decisions when you only have to choose between two or three insurance plans, instead of three hundred.

Ideally, you want to only have two or three good choices to choose from. Your brain has difficulty focusing on any more than that. Whenever you are looking at career choices, use some kind of criteria to narrow down your options to just two or three good options as quickly as possible. Anything more than that runs the risk of shutting down your thought process and producing an unsatisfying outcome.

## Working with your supervisor

A consistent theme of job satisfaction surveys is that employees need effective communication with management in order to be happy with their jobs.[8] This should make intuitive sense – how likely are you to be able to use your strengths effectively, work on issues you care about, or take advantage of new opportunities without support from your management?

Consider the examples of the following employees:[9]

Carla:

> I know that openly communicating with my supervisor builds trust in our relationship. I feel comfortable voicing my concerns when I feel overwhelmed or have personal issues. That way, if something is going to affect my performance, my supervisor won't incorrectly assume that I'm incapable of doing my job well.

John:

> Communicating with my supervisor and my coworkers keeps me informed on important updates and opportunities. Sometimes my supervisor tells me about projects that I might be interested in working on. When I talk to my coworkers about what I like to

*do, they sometimes ask me to help them out with things that I'm good at and also find interesting.*

Set up regular check-in times with your supervisor. By setting up meetings ahead of time, you can make sure that you are able to find time to talk about any issues you want to discuss. Use multiple modes of communication. Some people prefer to communicate in person; others prefer communicating over the phone or by email. Ask your supervisor which method they prefer, and let them know your preference too. Be flexible to changing the mode of communication based on changing work situations.

### 16 things happy people do to be happy at work

Finally, according to research conducted by TalentSmart, here are 16 habits that happy people tend to do to stay happy at work. These are great to review if you've found yourself dragging lately:[10]

| | | | |
|---|---|---|---|
| Remember that you are in charge of your own happiness | Don't obsess over things you can't control | Don't compare yourself to other people | Reward yourself |
| Exercise during the work week | Don't judge or gossip | Choose your battles wisely | Stay true to yourself |
| Clear the clutter | Give someone a hand | Let your strengths flow | Smile and laugh more |
| Stay away from negative people | Laugh at yourself | Cultivate an attitude of gratitude | Believe the best is yet to come |

# CHAPTER 5

# The Plan

*Mastery itself was the prize of the venture. – Winston Churchill*

On the very next page is a mostly blank piece of paper. There is a very feint outline of a figure in the middle of it. See how quickly you can find it.

Just kidding, there's nothing there. It's entirely blank – for now. This blank screen represents the next five years of your life. Nothing is written for you. Whatever you choose to do is completely up to you. Now, silently imagine, in as much detail as possible, who you are in five years. If you're 24-years-old, imagine who are you when you are 29-years-old. (If your five year plan is pretty well set, for example because you just started a degree program, then imagine who you are in 10 years instead. Pick an age that works for you.)

What are you doing?

What are you thinking?

Write it down on that blank page or screen, or use a separate blank sheet of paper (printer paper works best). Write down as much as you can. There is no wrong answer. Write what your gut says.

When you're finished, take your results from StrengthsFinder from Chapter 2. Read your number one strength.  Now, write down a list of as many ways as you can, given what you just wrote down, of what you can do to use that strength over the next five years. When you are done with strength number one, move on to strength number two, and so on until you have completed this exercise for all five strengths. Use the back of the blank page if necessary.

To provide an example, below are my top five strengths: Analytical, Learner, Input, Context, and Connectedness. Here is how I might have completed this exercise:

Who am I in five years? I am a program manager and a thought leader who helps others improve their lives. I have created a number of successful projects that have benefited others. I am earning a good salary and working reasonable hours, which has enabled me to maintain great health and build the social life that would help me meet a woman I love and possibly even marry.

What are my strengths, and how can I use them over the next five years?

1. **Analytical**. "People strong in the Analytical theme search for reasons and causes. They have the ability to think about all the factors that might affect a situation."[1]

How I could use my Analytical strength over the next five years:

- ❖ I could author more papers and articles in my job,[*] explaining why certain policies were or were not working. I could then share these writings with others to move them in the right direction, and build my reputation as a thought leader. I can incorporate interesting stories into my articles that I can enjoyably tell in social settings as well.

- ❖ I could record my predictions of the future to keep track of where I got them wrong, figure out why, and get better at it. I will use these predictions to determine what products I should create, and also to give advice for others planning their future as well.

2. **Learner**. "People strong in the Learner theme have a great desire to learn and want to continuously improve. In particular, the process of learning, rather than the outcome, excites them."[2]

How I could use my Learner strength over the next five years:

- ❖ I will take advanced training in anything related to my job that I think will grow in importance in the future. Since I plan for my job to involve program management and the web, I will train myself in web programming and management, technological trends, as well as fundamental

---

[*] The very research that helped me write this book.

skill areas in finance, accounting, personnel, and leadership.

3. **Input**. "People strong in the Input theme have a craving to know more. Often they like to collect and archive all kinds of information."[3]

How I could use my Input strength over the next five years:

❖ I will better keep track of the things I learn. I will keep a record of anything I write, for example, I will not throw it away. I will digitize everything using Dropbox so I do not have to feel compelled to throw anything away. I will pay to upgrade my Dropbox service so I do not feel compelled to delete any valuable information.

❖ I will make a daily habit of learning a fun fact about a random topic, and I will make a point to share my random fun facts with friends, family, and coworkers. I will be the "fun fact guy."

4. **Context**. "People strong in the Context theme enjoy thinking about the past. They understand the present by researching its history."[4]

How I could use my Context strength over the next five years:

❖ When I have reading time, I will focus on reading history. I will purchase non-fiction audio books and listen to them while I complete chores to increase the overall time I am using Context.

❖ When I meet people, I will focus on learning their history first, and think about how it helps me understand their present.

5. **Connectedness**. "People strong in the Connectedness theme have faith in the links between all things. They believe there are few coincidences and that almost every event has a reason."[5]

❖   I will make an effort to stay connected to friends and family as much as possible, checking in using Facebook and hosting gatherings for them to mix and mingle at. I will seek their counsel for important decisions.

❖   I will volunteer for assignments that I believe are helpful whenever possible even if I do not see an immediate benefit to them, because I know everything is connected and someone will benefit somewhere. I will seek out mentors and make an effort to meet them on their terms; I will express gratitude so that they can enjoy the mentoring experience as much as I benefit from it.

Finally, now that you have completed writing down ideas for all five of your strengths, what patterns do you see?

Underline anything you think overlaps. For example, under Connectedness I wrote that I should volunteer for assignments that might help others. Meanwhile, under Analytical, I wrote that I should write more. I could combine those two and say instead that "I should volunteer to write articles that might help others." I've now used two strengths in one task! I could go even further and add a third by saying, "I should volunteer to write articles that help others on topics that I need to learn more about, like web technology." Now I'm using three strengths! How might I add the other two strengths and use all five?

I could save my article to my Dropbox, and I could make sure that one of the paragraphs of my helpful web article is about history. Boom! Now I'm using all five strengths in one volunteer assignment. That sounds like a really fun assignment actually, I should get on that...

And that, you see, is the process of planning to your strengths. You will be so much more successful, and more effective and more excited, if you do this than if you simply did what others said you should do.

By using your strengths, it's about you and only you.

Now in completing this exercise you may have written down too many goals on your blank sheet of paper. Maybe you wrote down you want to get your PhD, and have two kids, and have a six-figure salary all within five years – and you haven't even finished your Bachelor's yet! I hate to break this to you, but that's probably not going to happen. Spend some time thinking about the various obstacles, like time or money, that could prevent you from accomplishing the goals in your five-year plan. Think of the trade-offs you can make. How many different paths can take you to accomplishing at least two or three of your goals? Which one seems less risky? More fun?

Remember – You can have everything in life, but you can't have everything at once.[†] You need to craft a *sequence*. What can you do in year one? And what can wait until year two, or year three? What can wait until 10 years down the road? What *can't* wait?

The exercise we are conducting is called critical visualization. It's a method taught to corporate executives, and a very effective one if done properly. The improper way to do it is the "wishful thinking" form of visualization, where you picture yourself sipping endless Mai Thais on the beach, making millions, but with no realistic plan for getting there.[‡] Research has shown that participants who are told to visualize attaining goals using the "wishful thinking" method end up attaining far fewer goals than those who are not told to do so. Wishful thinking visualizers report feeling less energetic as well. Instead, you must use critical visualization, where you consider obstacles you might encounter to achieving those goals, and then come up with realistic plans for addressing them.[6]

---

[†] This is a modified version of a quote from former Secretary of State Madeleine Albright: "Women can't do everything at the same time, we need to understand milestones in our lives come in segments."

[‡] As seen in the movie *Pain and Gain*.

If you fully completed this exercise, you should feel a sense of relief, empowerment, or both. You will not only feel a much greater sense of control over your destiny, but you will have the beginning of a real, written plan on how to get there, and one that includes new ideas that you probably had never thought of before. And by tying it to your StrengthsFinder results, your plan will be tailored to the particular talents that make *you* special.

### Creating the career map

Even if you're not one hundred percent sure what you want to do next, you must have a career map – something you can use to target training and opportunities. In the competitive job market, if you're not moving forward, you're falling behind. The good news is you can create a free career map at www.mycareeratva.va.gov to help get you started.

### Step 1 – Where are you?

The first step in creating your Career Map is stating where you are in your career. In this exercise, this refers to your current job title, but you will also want to keep in mind your student status, skills, education, and experience. As an example, on the next page you will find a federal government career map beginning as an entry-level Information Technology (IT) Specialist.

### Step 2 – Where are you going?

Determine where you want to go, then identify what you need to go from where you are to where you want to go. Usually this requires learning and demonstrating new skills, or earning new certifications or degrees. If you are creating a sample career map on MyCareer@VA (www.mycareeratva.va.gov), after selecting a current position, next click on any job title that comes up. Once you pick a target job, a career map connecting the two will populate on your screen. What this sample career map can do is show you what the required "Knowledge Areas," or skills, and education requirements are for various positions, which you will need to plan your own career. The career map can also direct you to recommended training courses; just click on the link under the "Career Guides" section to find those.

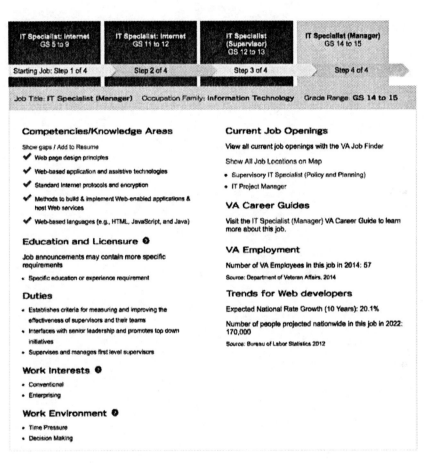

*Above is what the end of a career map looks like using the free MyCareer@VA tool (www.MyCareerAtVA.va.gov), a program that I used to lead. The above describes the senior management level position of an IT Specialist.*

## Job research

As I mentioned earlier, the sample career map tool doesn't include every position in its database. It is limited to positions in the federal government for one particular – though large – federal agency. As a result, you will want to familiarize yourself with other occupations in the public and private sectors as well. In the following two pages you will find employment statistics for the largest career fields in the United States, as well as the average salaries for each one, courtesy of the Federal Bureau of Labor Statistics and CareerInfoNet.org.[7]

Looking through these career fields personally brings back a lot of memories. Before starting my full-time career, I held part-time jobs in sales, and also worked as a cashier, office clerk, and food worker. I loved the experience they gave me; they taught me many invaluable skills that set me ahead of my peers when I finally did start my full-time career. You should definitely consider these other fields in the same way, especially if you're still a student. Consider taking on part-time jobs in fields that play to one of your strengths and absorb the invaluable training they can give you. Where possible, gravitate towards jobs that come with good training included. Not every organization provides training, but the best ones do.

**Top 50 Occupations with the Largest Employment**

Displaying Records 1 - 25 of 50          **Next 25 >**                              **Show All Records**

| # | Occupation | Employment 2012 | Earnings | Typical Education |
|---|---|---|---|---|
| 1 | Retail Salespersons | 4,447,000 | $ | Less than high school |
| 2 | Cashiers | 3,338,900 | $ | Less than high school |
| 3 | Office Clerks, General | 2,983,500 | $$ | High school diploma or equivalent |
| 4 | Combined Food Preparation and Serving Workers, Including Fast Food | 2,969,300 | $ | Less than high school |
| 5 | Registered Nurses | 2,711,500 | $$$$ | Associate's degree |
| 6 | Customer Service Representatives | 2,362,800 | $$ | High school diploma or equivalent |
| 7 | Waiters and Waitresses | 2,362,200 | $ | Less than high school |
| 8 | Secretaries and Administrative Assistants, Except Legal, Medical, and Executive | 2,324,400 | $$ | High school diploma or equivalent |
| 9 | Janitors and Cleaners, Except Maids and Housekeeping Cleaners | 2,324,000 | $ | Less than high school |
| 10 | Laborers and Freight, Stock, and Material Movers, Hand | 2,197,300 | $$ | Less than high school |
| 11 | General and Operations Managers | 1,972,700 | $$$$ | Bachelor's degree |
| 12 | Stock Clerks and Order Fillers | 1,807,200 | $ | Less than high school |
| 13 | Bookkeeping, Accounting, and Auditing Clerks | 1,799,800 | $$$ | High school diploma or equivalent |
| 14 | Heavy and Tractor-Trailer Truck Drivers | 1,701,500 | $$$ | Postsecondary non-degree award |
| 15 | First-Line Supervisors of Retail Sales Workers | 1,603,300 | $$$ | High school diploma or equivalent |
| 16 | Sales Representatives, Wholesale and Manufacturing, Except Technical and Scientific Products | 1,480,700 | $$$ | High school diploma or equivalent |
| 17 | Nursing Assistants | 1,479,800 | $$ | Postsecondary non-degree award |
| 18 | Maids and Housekeeping Cleaners | 1,434,600 | $ | Less than high school |
| 19 | First-Line Supervisors of Office and Administrative Support Workers | 1,418,100 | $$$ | High school diploma or equivalent |
| 20 | Elementary School Teachers, Except Special Education | 1,361,200 | $$$ | Bachelor's degree |
| 21 | Maintenance and Repair Workers, General | 1,325,100 | $$$ | High school diploma or equivalent |
| 22 | Childcare Workers | 1,312,700 | $ | High school diploma or equivalent |
| 23 | Accountants and Auditors | 1,275,400 | $$$$ | Bachelor's degree |
| 24 | Teacher Assistants | 1,223,400 | $$ | Some college, no degree |
| 25 | Personal Care Aides | 1,190,600 | $ | Less than high school |

**Next 25 >**

**National Data Source:** Bureau of Labor Statistics, Office of Occupational Statistics and Employment Projections

*Table produced by CareerInfoNet.org*

## Top 50 Occupations with the Largest Employment

Displaying Records 26 - 50 of 50　　　**< Previous 25**　　　**Show All Records**

| # | Occupation | Employment 2012 | Earnings | Typical Education |
|---|---|---|---|---|
| 26 | Landscaping and Groundskeeping Workers | 1,124,900 | $$ | Less than high school |
| 27 | Security Guards | 1,074,300 | $$ | High school diploma or equivalent |
| 28 | Construction Laborers | 1,071,100 | $$ | Less than high school |
| 29 | Team Assemblers | 1,031,800 | $$ | High school diploma or equivalent |
| 30 | Cooks, Restaurant | 1,024,100 | $ | Less than high school |
| 31 | Receptionists and Information Clerks | 1,006,700 | $$ | High school diploma or equivalent |
| 32 | Secondary School Teachers, Except Special and Career/Technical Education | 955,800 | $$$ | Bachelor's degree |
| 33 | Farmers, Ranchers, and Other Agricultural Managers | 930,600 | $$$$ | High school diploma or equivalent |
| 34 | Carpenters | 901,200 | $$$ | High school diploma or equivalent |
| 35 | Home Health Aides | 875,100 | $ | Less than high school |
| 36 | Executive Secretaries and Executive Administrative Assistants | 873,900 | $$$ | High school diploma or equivalent |
| 37 | First-Line Supervisors of Food Preparation and Serving Workers | 848,500 | $$ | High school diploma or equivalent |
| 38 | Light Truck or Delivery Services Drivers | 841,600 | $$ | High school diploma or equivalent |
| 39 | Food Preparation Workers | 807,800 | $ | Less than high school |
| 40 | Lawyers | 759,800 | $$$$ | Doctoral or professional degree |
| 41 | Licensed Practical and Licensed Vocational Nurses | 738,400 | $$$ | Postsecondary non-degree award |
| 42 | Management Analysts | 718,700 | $$$$ | Bachelor's degree |
| 43 | Automotive Service Technicians and Mechanics | 701,100 | $$$ | High school diploma or equivalent |
| 44 | Shipping, Receiving, and Traffic Clerks | 695,500 | $$ | High school diploma or |
| 45 | Packers and Packagers, Hand | 666,900 | $ | Less than high school |
| 46 | Police and Sheriff's Patrol Officers | 653,800 | $$$ | High school diploma or equivalent |
| 47 | Middle School Teachers, Except Special and Career/Technical Education | 614,400 | $$$ | Bachelor's degree |
| 48 | Software Developers, Applications | 613,000 | $$$$ | Bachelor's degree |
| 49 | Hairdressers, Hairstylists, and Cosmetologists | 611,200 | $$ | Postsecondary non-degree award |
| 50 | Farmworkers and Laborers, Crop, Nursery, and Greenhouse | 596,800 | $ | Less than high school |

**< Previous 25**

**National Data Source:** Bureau of Labor Statistics, Office of Occupational Statistics and Employment Projections

*Table produced by CareerInfoNet.org*

## Worst Case / Best Case Method

Very often in career planning you are faced with at least two good, but not perfect, options that can determine your fate. No pressure, right? Well it can be very difficult to think through these and make a good decision, and you don't want to become unnecessarily stressed or, heaven forbid, turn to a coin to decide your fate.[§] In this case, I recommend you use my *Worst Case / Best Case* method, which I derived using a theory from economics known as Opportunity Cost – *what opportunity am I giving up when I make (or don't make) a choice?*:

| Over the next five years Sarah can: | Worst case | Best case |
|---|---|---|
| Option 1: Go to law school for three years and then corporate law for two years | Earn +$100,000 total in a mid-level job (deduct -$150,000 in student debt) | Become a respected corporate lawyer on her way to earning a *high six-figure salary* in a high-level job |
| Option 2: Get a community based job for all five years | Earn +$250,000 total in a mid-level job | Become a respected community leader / manager *earning less than a six-figure salary* |

The *Worst Case / Best Case* method is a simple chart where you list the *likeliest* worst-case and best-case scenarios for each serious career option you have in front of you. In the example

---

[§] There is one useful method for coin flips that a friend taught me: the next time you have a tough choice, and if all other methods fail (including my *Worst Case / Base Case* method), go ahead and try flipping that coin. Then see how you feel when it turns up heads or tails. If you cringe, then the coin made the wrong choice, just go ahead and pick the opposite. If instead, after the coin comes up heads (or tails), you feel a sense of relief, then the coin actually made the right choice, and you can now confidently go with that. This method helps you reveal what it is that you truly desire.

above, I use the example of Sarah, who has two opportunities – one to go to law school and then to a corporate law job, and another option to stay and work in her community. Each option will take the next five years. Here, Sarah's worst case scenario clearly favors her staying and working in her community; she will make more money since she won't have student debt to worry about. However, the *best case* scenario is a bit more complicated. Here she must choose *if it is worth the risk* of spending all of that money on law school to have *the chance* of becoming the corporate lawyer earning a high six-figure salary. It's a risk – no one is guaranteed a job with a high six figure salary no matter what their education is, and she could always fail to land that prestigious job after going to school, or simply quit after discovering she didn't enjoy it as much as she had hoped.**

Not only is Option 1 risky, but the best case scenario for Option 2 is also very appealing. If Sarah is most passionate about her community and is ok with the trade-off of making less salary so that she could be closer to friends and family (and perhaps work more reasonable hours, important for starting a family), then the question becomes less difficult – she should take Option 2. She will be happy in either best case scenario, and the worst case scenario of Option 2 is much better.

Now let's flip it around and instead, let's say Sarah's passion is not her community at all, it's really traveling. She actually isn't terribly interested in working in her community because, well, let's say she doesn't have many ties there anymore; most of her friends and family have since moved on. In addition to that, traveling as much as she dreams of requires a high salary. Because of these new facts, the best case for Option 2 would actually leave Sarah dreadfully unhappy, even though the worst case for Option 2 is still a bit better than the worst case for Option 1 (that law debt would hurt her travel budget in the short term). In this alternative scenario, she should definitely take the plunge and go for Option

** This was President Barack Obama's experience after graduating from Harvard Law.

1, the law school / corporate lawyer route, because she will be guaranteed to be unhappy with Option 2 *even if everything works out perfectly*. In this alternative scenario, she's not risking anything by choosing Option 1 – she really has nothing to lose, and only her happiness to gain.

## How do I switch to an entirely new career?

If you've determined that switching to an entirely new career is right for you, it will be difficult but you have a few options ahead of you. One option is to go back to school, for more on that option please read the chapter on going to (back) to school. Another option is to begin shading your work and training towards your new desired career field, then, when you're ready, take a new job in that new career field. This avenue is much less costly than going back to school, though you may still have to downgrade your salary depending on your skill level and the job market.

### Preparing for an entirely new career

Once you've decided to begin branching out, you'll need to heavily invest in research, training, and on-the-job experience in your new field. If you've decided you want to become a computer programmer for example, you could do the following:

- ❖ *Research*. Read and listen to prominent experts in the field. For example, you could listen to podcasts from the 5by5.tv podcast network or from Marco Arment of the Accidental Tech Podcast show. You could peruse the famous blog DaringFireball.net and explore software and graphic design skills as well by listening to Mike Monteiro's famous "F--- You, Pay Me" talk[8] or reading his book, *Design Is a Job*.[9] The point of research is to understand what your new life would be like in this career.

- ❖ *Training*. Create an account at Lynda.com and take some of the great courses they have to introduce you to new subjects in your field. Feel energized by the material and the ideas they are empowering you to create. Search Google and YouTube for free tutorials as well. Remember though, while free training is great, always prioritize quality training – quality training is truly invaluable, and you should be willing to pay for it. Enroll in an in-person training course or conference if possible to get the best results and enhance your network as well.

❖ *On-the-job experience.* Volunteer for or propose projects that allow you to use skills in your new career field in the job that you have right now. Does your office need a new website? Volunteer to program it for them. Does it want a mobile app? See what it will take you to create it. If you need a little professional help see what that would cost and request a budget. Figure out what it takes to create something good and start producing something you can be proud of.

Before you know it, you will be the _____ that you want to be.

### What should I tell my supervisor?

Though he or she might not always know it, your supervisor is responsible for the development of your career just like you are. It is a partnership to complete your career plan together. Like any good partnership, the outcome should be a win-win for you and your organization. The career plan you develop with your supervisor should be shorter than the five year plan you completed earlier, it should generally be focused only on the upcoming year (though you can certainly stretch it into a longer three or five-year plan if it makes sense for you and your supervisor).

In this partnership, your role is to understand how well your skills match what you need to complete your goals; to identify training opportunities that will help you achieve your goals; and to assess your progress. Your supervisor's role is to help you assess your strengths and developmental needs; to provide opportunities to discuss and plan your development; help you identify training opportunities; make sure that your training opportunities align with your goals; and ensure that your goals align with the organization's objectives.[10]

Once you've developed a career plan with these in mind, set a time for reviewing your plan with your supervisor. Your supervisor is a valuable resource for your career planning and can help you explore possibilities you may not have considered. Your supervisor will also need to approve of any new on-the-job duties or training you want to include in your current job.

The purpose of this meeting with your supervisor is to come away with a comprehensive plan for your development. This includes goals as well as new actions that will help you pursue your goals. You will have the opportunity to share what you have brainstormed and your supervisor will help you explore possibilities you may not have considered. Afterward, be sure to schedule a follow-up meeting to review and adjust your plan as needed and check on your progress.

### Making your career conversation a success

Bring your development needs, goals, and potential resources to the discussion. Be open to your supervisor's feedback and suggestions. Choose a time when both of you can stay focused on the conversation without distractions. Place timelines on your goals and set specific guidelines for follow-up. Schedule a follow-up meeting to review your progress.

### Predicting the future

The future is inextricably bound to discussions of your career. Where is your industry headed? Will there be jobs in your favorite career field? Will they be making more money than they are now? Less? Should I invest my time in this skill, this software program, this company, or this strategy? You may think – surely this is the job of an analyst! And you would be right. Then you must also think – I'll read what the best analysts are thinking, and I will be able to get this right myself. That will certainly help you, but you would still be missing out.

The best wisdom I can offer you on reading the tealeaves comes from James Surowiecki's *The Wisdom of Crowds*. Surowiecki begins with the following tale from 1906:

> As he walked through the exhibition that day, Galton came across a weight-judging competition. A fat ox had been selected and placed on display, and members of a gathering crowd were lining up to place wagers on the weight of the ox...For sixpence, you could buy a stamped and numbered ticket, where you filled in your name, your address, and your estimate. The best guesses would receive prizes.
>
> Galton was interested in figuring out what the "average voter" was capable of because he wanted to prove that the average voter was capable of very little. So...when the contest was over and the prizes had been awarded...he added all the contestants' estimates, and calculated the [average] of the group's guesses...[and] Galton was wrong. The crowd had guessed that the ox, after it had been slaughtered and dressed, would weigh 1,197 pounds. After it had been slaughtered and dressed, the ox weighed 1,198 pounds. In other words, the crowd's judgment was essentially perfect.[11]

Galton's experiment was not the only time a crowd's guess had proven so effective a predictor. Surowiecki documents dozens of examples of this effect, also known as "crowdsourcing" today, where the crowd time and again beats the experts in making predictions. I use this method when I go shopping for wine. I try and buy the wine that is almost sold out. Bad wine doesn't sell out – the crowd is (generally) too smart for that.

Sometimes the crowd is wrong, and if you know the crowd is wrong, you can do very well for yourself by following the advice of someone who is right. But what Surowiecki reveals is that we tend to overestimate the power of experts. When in doubt, if you truly do not know which expert to follow, don't just ask another expert. See what *everyone* is doing, what *everyone* is recommending, experts and non-experts alike. Time and again, that approach will tend to beat even the best expert. This is, not coincidentally, the same reason why this very book includes information from so many diverse fields of research; diversity and breadth of thought is essential for forming the best decisions.

# CHAPTER 6

# The Routine

*Even a small thing takes a few years. To do anything of magnitude takes at least five years, more likely seven or eight. –Steve Jobs*

For the first 150 years of American history, literature that described success focused on character ethics – principles like integrity, humility, courage, patience, and modesty. Early autobiographies of the Founding Fathers, Stephen R. Covey writes in the immensely successful book *The 7 Habits of Highly Effective People*, were generally written in this way.[1] Then the winds shifted. As Covey details, after World War I, the literature focused on success shifted from character ethics to focusing on your personality, and how to manipulate it to get what you want. Covey writes:

> *Some of this philosophy was expressed in inspiring and sometimes valid maxims such as 'Your attitude determines your altitude,' Smiling wins more friends than frowning,' and 'Whatever the mind of man can conceive and believe it can achieve'… Other parts of the personality approach were clearly manipulative, even deceptive, encouraging people to use techniques to get other people to like them, or to fake interest in the hobbies of others to get out of them what they wanted, or to use the 'power look,' or to intimidate their way through life.*[2]

You're probably familiar with this approach. You see it on bookshelves, TV infomercials, and internet ads every day. You're probably also very skeptical of this approach. That's good, because it doesn't work.

"The glitter of the Personality Ethic," Covey explains, "is that there is some quick and easy way to achieve quality of life – personal effectiveness and rich, deep relationships with other people – without going through the natural process of work and growth that makes it possible."[3]

No, success is not a get-rich-quick scheme. Some lucky people do get rich quick, or are born into wealth, but that doesn't necessarily make them happy. Happiness comes from the kind of success you cultivate through your Center, your character, your plan – and your routine.

Your routine will be the steps that lead you to your greatness. Your routine isn't about getting your job done per se, it's much greater than that. It's about cultivating the character that Covey describes, and creating the framework that will enable you to act effectively.

Think of everything in this chapter like a practice for a big game – every day is a new day to get your shots, your moves, your rhythm just a bit sharper, to perfect them just a bit more. If you are not working on nearly all of these every single day going forward, even if it is just for a few moments, you are doing something wrong.

### Covey's 7 Habits

The 7 Habits you will be using are:

* ❖ *Be Proactive.* As Henry David Thoreau wrote, "I know of no more encouraging fact than the unquestionable ability of man to elevate his life by conscious endeavor."

* ❖ *Begin with the End in Mind.* Before undertaking any endeavor, visualize the ending. Screenwriters like to say that a good movie ending is worth 10 great beginnings. The same is true of your projects. Do you seek applause? Financial gain? To change someone's behavior?

* ❖ *Put First Things First.* "Things which matter most must never be at the mercy of things which matter least." - Goethe

* ❖ *Think Win/Win.* If you can come up with a solution that benefits you and someone else, there are almost no limits to what you can achieve. Conversely, if it requires someone else to lose for it to work, you can play that trick only so many times before it runs dry.

* ❖ *Seek First to Understand, Then to Be Understood.* "The heart has its reasons which reason knows not of." – Pascal.

❖ *Synergize.* The whole is greater than the parts.

❖ *Sharpen the Saw.* Every day is practice for your great day. Get better, faster, sharper.

## Ethics

> *Man has a natural aptitude for virtue; but the perfection of virtue must be acquired by man by means of some kind of training.* – *Saint Thomas Aquinas*

In the 1970's, Ron Howard was working as a decision-analysis consultant. A defense contractor was asked by the federal government to analyze which fighter plane the U.S. Air Force should choose for its fleet. The winner of this analysis would win a contract worth millions, and due to an oversight, the same contractor conducting the analysis was also producing a fighter plane that was competing for the award. It was no surprise how this contractor wanted their "analysis" to turn out – if the report said their plane was best, it would earn them a whole lot of money. So the contractor offered Howard the job to produce the report and let him know exactly what he was getting paid for: "Of course, we all know how the analysis will come out," the defense contractor told Ron. [4]

Ron was caught surprised by the ethical dilemma he was faced with. He was being tempted to take the job, and the money, and skip a professional, thorough analysis. Howard "just needed to say yes to manipulating the results," he later wrote, "and the contract was his." Of course, if he were to accept and violate his professional ethics, he would also be putting his entire career, his future, at risk.

Ron turned down the job, but it taught him an important lesson: to always be prepared for those career-threatening challenges and to learn how to be aware of them and what to do when faced with them. In the book he co-wrote, *Ethics for the Real*

*World: Creating a Personal Code to Guide Decisions in Work and Life,* Howard and Clinton Korver provide a four-phased process to help you prepare to navigate these challenges:

- ❖ *First*, develop an awareness of ethical temptation and compromise as it relates to your career choice. Where have others stumbled in the path you wish to take? It's much easier to make a mistake if you're not even aware that mistake exists in the first place.

- ❖ *Second*, learn how to use ethical logic and principles to foster clear thinking. Identify and remind yourself of the principles that drive you. Make them a part of your routine.

- ❖ *Third*, develop an ethical code for making effective, efficient, life-enhancing decisions. Become skilled and *decisive* in your ethical choices.

- ❖ *Fourth*, strive to not simply do the "right" thing, but learn how to do the *best* thing in any given situation, and be willing to fight for it.

### Your schedule

Your schedule is the single most important aspect of your productivity. *How* you use it is *everything*. If your days are just happening without any rhyme or reason, you're wasting *something*. What it is, you don't know – you could be wasting your strengths, your passion, your opportunity.

Every day you should spend *at least a moment* thinking about what your schedule is and what it ought to be. You should build time for each habit or skill you want to build. You should also reserve time for the things your body and mind need.

- ❖ Your body needs sun – reserve time for sunlight.

- ❖ Your body needs to eat, sleep, and relax. Reserve time for those.

❖ Your mind needs to learn, to do, to play. If you can learn during your working hours, do it! If you can't, build it into your free time somehow. If you can make learning fun for yourself, you've just killed two birds with one stone.

❖ Your body needs to exercise. Seven minutes is fine. Of course, more is better. If you can exercise while working (walk and talk!) or learning (listening to an audiobook), even better!

Etc. etc. As you will learn in the chapter on saving time (skip ahead if you're fretting about time), you have more time than you think. Spend it wisely.

### Your calendar

Your calendar is a technical solution to managing your schedule. It is *not* your schedule. Your schedule is your life – your work as well as your sleep, your exercise, your time with your family. Your calendar is a means of managing these. Because of this, an effective calendar is critical to an effective life – whether you manage it for yourself, or someone else manages it for you.

The simplest rule is to only have one calendar and to manage it carefully. Don't overbook, don't promise to meet with someone without recording it on your calendar, don't make technical errors with your calendar software that embarrass you in front of people you care about. Pick one calendar and use it *extremely well*. It doesn't matter which software you use. I mainly used Microsoft Outlook because that is what my office used, and you better believe I became a master of Outlook's calendar function, I can run circles around just about anyone. Because it was the tool that I use to manage essentially what is my life (my schedule), I make it a point to know its capabilities and weaknesses very well. And you should too, for whichever software solution you choose.

### Create a "My Career" computer folder

There are many documents essential to your career – keep them stored safely, and electronically, where you can access them in a moment's notice. Include resumes, cover letters, documents for applications, letters of recommendation you've received or written for others, school diplomas, training certificates, random ideas, your career plans or maps, draft articles or diagrams for projects, networking information, events, business card designs, and anything else that is a part of your career development. Every minute you spend searching for something later is a minute wasted, so invest the time to keep yourself organized in advance and save yourself the trouble. Keep a back-up of this folder in a secured cloud account too (I use Dropbox), and don't ever trust information that is *only* stored on *one* physical computer. It will eventually die, and you don't want it to take your critical information with it.

### Your work space

As described in the chapter on passion, your work and home environments are extremely important to your happiness and productivity. Better environments produce more passionate people. People who are surrounded by environments with jagged edges, shoddy workmanship, or clutter – the anti-Feng Shui, are less productive.[5]

Use this to your advantage. Take a few minutes out of your day, perhaps those times when you need to clear your head or take a break, to make marginal improvements to your office or home environments. Improve the colors. Colors have effects – green increases innovative thinking.[6] Consider using them. Clutter increases stress, mistakes, and reduces productivity – clean it out. As does poor air quality,[7] which an air filter can help fix. These are just a few of the many, small opportunities that can add up to great improvements in your life.

## Your fitness

The single most important aspect of improving your fitness is something I mentioned earlier – your schedule. Whether it is seven minutes, fifteen minutes, or more – if you can schedule *some* amount of time for exercise every day, you will see improvement.

I'm an "F" student when it comes to exercise. I can barely accomplish half of the exercise goals I set out for myself. But today I am a frequent exerciser and in terrific physical condition – even though that has not changed. So how did I do it?

I used to believe that I needed to be great at exercising, like my father (a marathon runner) to be healthy. I needed to run five to ten miles, lift hundreds of weights, every day. Like my father. But whenever I would try, my body wasn't used to it, and I would fail. I would start off with very intense workouts and then need days to recover. By the time I recovered, I had forgotten about it and already settled back into my old routine.

Then, I settled for good enough. I decided I would just go to the gym for an hour every day and do whatever I felt like, even if it was hardly anything at all. And I did, more or less. I would skip occasionally and end up only going to about half of the gym sessions I scheduled for myself (my "F" rate on full display).  But even at that "F" rate, I was still working out for about an hour at moderate intensity 3-4 times a week. And I saw fantastic results in just a few months time. Guess what I did next? I started to do more.

And you will too. Just get it into your schedule, and make the accommodations for your own strengths, passion, and opportunity. Don't run if you hate running. Lift weights instead. Don't stress if you miss a gym day – just schedule enough that you can afford to. Just like your career, you have a fitness Center too. Make it work for you.

## Your sleep

You write emails drunk. You go to school drunk. You go to work drunk. You probably do, and have done, just about everything, drunk, without even realizing it.

Maybe you've never actually done any of these activities under the influence of alcohol, but I would be willing to bet you have done all of these while sleep deprived. As it turns out, being sleep deprived can be just as bad as being under the influence of alcohol. Stay awake longer than 18 consecutive hours and your reaction speed, short-term and long-term memory, ability to focus, decision-making capacity, math processing, cognitive speed, and spatial orientation all start to suffer. Cut sleep back to five or six hours a night for several days in a row, and the accumulated sleep deficit magnifies these negative effects. Sleep deprivation has been implicated in all kinds of physical maladies, too, from high blood pressure to obesity.[8]

Stay awake for a full 24 hours without sleep, or go a week with only four or five hours of sleep, and your level of impairment is equivalent to someone with a .1% blood alcohol level – enough to land a DUI.

Sleep deprivation doesn't just harm your work. It kills. In 2002, Israel Lane Joubert killed his wife and five of his six children when he fell asleep at the wheel; he was driving home from a family reunion and was hoping to be back in time for work the next day. A man in Florida is serving a 15-year prison sentence for killing three people when he failed to stop at a red light. He was working – driving the company car – and had been awake for thirty hours.

The scariest part of sleep deprivation is that it's often seen as a badge of honor in the workplace. The two examples I just gave were both *driving for work*, either to get there or while on the clock. From 2005-2009, drowsy driving was involved in 416,000 accidents, killing more than 5,000 people. How many of them were induced by their work? I don't know, but don't let a phony sense of honor in your workplace, or your school, make you think sleep deprivation is right. It is not.

### Life hacks

There are a lot of small techniques, often called "life hacks," that you can use on a daily basis to improve your energy. My favorite is to use an app called SleepCycle that monitors your sleep and adjusts your alarm clock to ensure you wake up when you're in light sleep (as opposed to REM, deep sleep) to help you wake up feeling refreshed instead of groggy. Who likes to feel groggy in the morning? (I also find taking a bite of an apple immediately after waking up cures morning grogginess.) Another neat trick for those who like to read from a device like an iPad or Kindle late at night is to wear orange glasses, which block blue light and improve your sleep. As you'll see in the next chapter, different foods of course have different effects on your energy and mood – wheat and refined sugar worsen it, greens and natural sugars (i.e. fruits) improve it, as does drinking a lot of water. There are many more out there, so keep an eye out for them. Even the smallest changes in your daily routine, if you repeat them enough times, can have enormous impacts on your overall career.

# CHAPTER 7

# Do I need a mentor? A partner?

*Man is by nature a social animal. – Aristotle*

Many people view their careers as an individual effort, but for the vast majority of professionals that is just not how careers work. People by and large work in teams, and succeed by learning from mentors and forming partnerships with colleagues to accomplish goals together. This isn't an accident, it's how human beings are wired. Humans do not function well in isolation. Isolation has been linked to such maladies as high blood pressure, high cholesterol, cigarette smoking, obesity, and lack of exercise.[1] Partnerships, meanwhile, have the opposite effect:[2]

> *The more good partnerships you have in your life, the more likely you are to say that you experienced the feeling of enjoyment much of the day yesterday, that you recently learned something interesting, and that you've been doing a lot of smiling and laughing – all key measures of your happiness. Even having one strong partnership increases your well-being over those who have none…In the workplace, employees with just one collaborative relationship are 29 percent more likely to say they will stay with their company for the next year and 42 percent more likely to intend to remain with their current employer for their entire career, compared to those with no partnerships. Those who feel well-teamed with one or more colleagues are substantially more engaged at work. They generate higher customer scores and better safety, retention, creativity, productivity, and profitability for the business – and a greater level of happiness for themselves…When asked how many strong alliances they have, most people say they have just a few, even though the highest levels of happiness and employee engagement kick in when a person has 5 to 10 good alliances.*

You should *always* be seeking out successful partnerships. Be strategic, don't partner with just anyone. But always have an eye open for who might be your next great partner. Once you have established a partnership, take care to ensure you are meeting these eight elements that Rodd Wagner and Gale Muller have identified as essential components of successful partnerships:[3]

- ❖ *Complementary strengths.* "The same man cannot be skilled in everything; each has his special excellence." – Euripides

- ❖ *A common mission.* "A friendship founded on business is better than a business founded on friendship." – John D. Rockefeller

- ❖ *Fairness.* "There is no such thing as justice in the abstract; it is merely a compact between men." – Epicurius

- ❖ *Trust.* "For when the One Great Scorer comes to mark against your name, He writes – not that you won or lost – but how you played the Game." – U.S. sportswriter Grantland Rice

- ❖ *Acceptance.* "Admiration, n. Our polite recognition of another's resemblance to ourselves." – Ambrose Bierce

- ❖ *Forgiveness.* "He that studieth revenge keepeth his own wounds green, which otherwise would heal and do well." – John Milton

- ❖ *Communicating.* "The more elaborate our means of communication, the less we communicate." – Joseph Priestley

- ❖ *Unselfishness.*

  *I've always hated the danger part of climbing, and it's great to come down again because it's safe. But there is something about building up a comradeship – that I still believe is the greatest of all feats – and sharing in the dangers with your company of peers. It's the intense effort, the giving of everything you've got. It's really a very pleasant sensation. – Sir Edmund Hillary*

Mentors, as a result, are incredibly important. The mistake people make with mentors is that they forget that mentors are only as important as their strengths. You need partners to survive and succeed, and mentors are among the most important of those partners. But you will never find one mentor to rule them all. The reality is you will need many mentors to succeed throughout the course of your life. Never assume that one mentor is enough, or that one mentor is qualified to get you the knowledge you need. But one is better than none, and more is better than a few. Seek out their counsel regularly and let them know that their advice and experience are valued. Repay the favor by providing them your own advice and assistance in those areas that you are relatively stronger in.

## Mentoring tips[4]

At every stage in your career (and your life), you should be trying to meet all of the following conditions: have a *mentor* who is more experienced than you in a field you are interested in; have at least one *partner* who has similar experience for at least one new project; and mentor at least one other person who is *less* experienced than you. It is the right thing to do, and it will also make you more effective and build a larger network for yourself.

In many of the hundreds of interviews I have read and conducted with successful professionals, a consistent theme is how enormously beneficial it was to their success to have a great mentor. This should make intuitive sense. Working with a mentor can help you get feedback on your plans and ideas; teach you aspects about the organization or industry (or people) you can't find elsewhere; better understand your strengths and explore your potential; make a smoother transition into your job; grow your network; and point you in the direction of new opportunities. Mentors are at *worst* helpful, and at best invaluable.

To find a mentor, just ask. It's really that simple. See if you can meet the potential mentor a few times to get a sense if they would be good fit for you. Then, just ask. Someone either can or can't mentor you, and if they can't, you need to find that out right away so you can find someone who else can.

Once you have a mentor, it will take some work to keep the relationship going. Keep in mind that it's *your* career and your responsibility to direct the mentoring relationship and the conversations you have with your mentor. Don't wait for your mentor to contact you (even if they often will), take it upon yourself to schedule the meetings, have a clear time commitment you both agree on (my favorite is to meet once every three weeks) and come ready to discuss specific topics. Don't be shy – anything you wrote down about your plan from that chapter in the book should be great fodder for discussing with your mentor. If you run out of specifics to discuss, think of open-ended questions to ask your mentor, such as their opinions on various issues that may have opportunities for your career. The time you have together is finite, so try to use it as productively as you can. You should be friendly and get to know each other; use chit-chat about friends, family, and the weather as dressing for the conversation – but don't let it always *become* the conversation if you have other, more pertinent items to discuss. Be very respectful of their time, they are volunteering it after all, so don't let meetings run over time unless they make it clear they want it to. Listen carefully, and ask for and gratefully accept any criticism they will share with you. Don't forget to take notes too; it is actually probably the highest form of respect you can pay a mentor.

This relationship described above is considered a "formal" mentoring relationship. You typically won't have many of these due to the time commitment required, but you can have many informal mentoring relationships too. Anytime you ask someone more experienced than you for advice you are receiving informal mentoring. Informal mentors are an excellent way to expand your network, since they provide an easy method to keep the relationship active (seeking advice), people *enjoy* giving advice, and you can use that advice to do your work better. While this sounds incredibly obvious, you would be surprised how little people use their network for informal mentoring, probably due to excessive shyness, pride, or forgetfulness. When I contact my informal mentors I can tell they don't receive those requests very often – and I know I don't either.

Becoming a mentor has its own benefits as well. Not only will you help someone else's professional development, you can also develop your coaching, listening and counseling skills. It's also another excellent way to grow your network.

### Role models – the career cheat code

Many times, the best mentor is the one you never meet. Before you ever commit to becoming great in a particular field, you should always start by understanding what it took to be great for those who accomplished it first. Read (auto-)biographies, interviews, and blog posts, or listen to podcasts or audio books (as many as you can) from people whose careers you would love to have. There is no substitute from learning from the best. You may never even get to meet the best, but that's ok – modern technology makes it incredibly easy to learn from them anyway. A wealth of knowledge *tailored to your career* is just waiting, *begging* for you all around the internet, as well as in bookstores and public libraries in your neighborhood. If you love your field, you will love learning about those who are great in it too.

Other times, you may actually meet great role models for your career without even knowing it. It takes a careful eye to identify a great role model in person, as well as practice in active listening and asking effective questions. I find people are just as likely to dismiss a person they know as a role model as they are to emulate them. To give just one example, while I am not an expert at many things, I do know a few things about writing, career training, and website management – these three functions happen to be three functions I do professionally at a very large scale. I deliver presentations, talks, and lectures on these three subjects to complete strangers on a regular basis. Complete strangers that will listen attentively and take notes on what I say, because that is what you do when a credentialed speaker comes to visit. But something funny happens if the person first gets to know me outside of these settings – I usually consider myself lucky if I can finish a sentence, let alone have the person take notes. At an unusually high frequency, people of this same audience that would normally listen attentively and take notes when in the audience of one of my presentations, would instead prefer to lecture, rather than listen, to what an experienced professional has to say in person.

I don't take it personally, it's everyone's choice to listen to whomever they want to; sometimes it's even enlightening to hear what a non-expert has to say about various topics that I work in. But even still, I frequently meet people like this that I think could really *improve* at their jobs if they just listened more to good advice from successful role models.  And when I think that this person is actively harming their career by not doing so, I get sad. I used to be this way myself, and it wasn't until I stopped and instead tried actively listening to anyone who could be an effective role model for me did I truly start to learn, eliminating significant mistakes from my professional life. I don't follow every bit word for word, but now I at least give it a fair hearing before offering my own opinions.

My reason is a selfish one – you can save *so much time* learning from role models if you never have to repeat the same mistakes they had to in order to get to where they are. You can skip right past those mistakes and move beyond even your greatest role model. A great role model is like the ultimate video game cheat code – you can skip entire levels of learning by simply following the right advice.

# CHAPTER 8

# Health

*But I say to you that when you work you fulfil a part of earth's furthest dream, assigned to you when that dream was born, And in keeping yourself with labour you are in truth loving life, And to love life through labour is to be intimate with life's inmost secret.*
*– Khalil Gibran*

I once interviewed career development expert Alice Muellerweiss, a former government executive and now a business owner and CEO, on what she believed her secret was to long-term career success. Her answer? It was her dedication to her health. A former soldier, once she left the Army she increasingly became more sick and sluggish, and felt that her lower energy and productivity were letting down those who depended on her. That motivation to be there when she was needed provided her with the motivation to become more disciplined about her health, which in turn gave her the energy to accomplish her greatest career successes. As she explains in her book, *It's Your Career:*[1]

> When I was active-duty military, I was in excellent shape and physically fit. During the first four years after leaving the military, however, my level of fitness gradually declined... I was a full-time employee...I was also going to school at night, raising my children, a wife, and involved in community activities...I had a full schedule and made no time for exercise. Consequently, I gained quite a bit of weight...I felt sluggish, my energy level was lower [and] I took more sick days...My diet consisted of pizza, cheeseburgers, or anything I could get through a drive-through window...Regardless of my schedule, I have been consistent with exercise and healthy eating since 2002...If career growth is important to you, and if you want to grow in your current job or change jobs, take stock and make the necessary adjustments.

### Sad and not knowing why

Americans in the workplace are increasingly sad, even depressed, without really knowing why. This may affect you or someone you know. Psychologist Stephen Ilardi, an expert on the subject, has written extensively about the phenomenon.[2] What is well known is that depression has been on the rise for decades, with approximately seventy million Americans currently affected. What many are not aware of is that the only known group of Americans that has not been affected by this trend is the Amish. And while this trend has affected people across the world as their countries have increasingly adopted the American lifestyle, this trend has *not* appeared in populations that have not. Depression does not exist at all, for example, in hunter-gatherer bands like the Kaluli people of New Guinea. What is it about the modern American lifestyle that has increased the worldwide risk of depression? Ilardi has documented six major protective lifestyle elements that our ancestors, like the Kaluli people of New Guinea, used to have that we often neglect today, but which we require to be biologically and psychologically happy. Be sure to incorporate each of these elements into your life to ensure you are as happy and productive as possible:[3]

- ❖ *Dietary omega-3 fatty acids* (fish oil).

- ❖ *Engaging activity.*

- ❖ *Physical exercise.*

- ❖ *Sunlight exposure* (or vitamin D3 supplements).

- ❖ *Social support.*

- ❖ *Sleep.*

I've incorporated each of these into my daily routine, including taking daily omega-3 and vitamin D3 supplements, and have noticed dramatic improvements in my life. My worst days – which used to occur during the winter when I typically had low sunlight, longer working hours, and poorer diet – *no longer exist.* This has not only significantly improved my work, but also my relationships and overall happiness. We already discussed the importance of engaging activity, social support, and sleep in earlier chapters. In this chapter, we'll discuss tips for diet and exercise.

## Exercise

You can make it work for you, even if you only have a few minutes to spare. Consider Alice's experience:[4]

> *I remember a time when I wouldn't work out unless I had a solid hour...in my first executive position, I had an entirely different*

*view....I quickly realized that I could do 20 minutes of running or walking in the morning and 20 minutes after coming home[.] Breaking up my fitness activities allowed me to create balance with my family.*

If even 20 minutes is a bit too much, you can get results with as little as 7 minutes a day if you are consistent and do it at a high-enough level of intensity. Many of my workouts are between just 10 and 20 minutes long, the important thing to me is that I just do whatever I can. You can too. Consider the popular *7 Minute Workout* routine for days when you don't have much time or energy, and save your longer workouts for days when you're schedule is more open and you're feeling up to it. Exercise, as you will see, is actually the easiest part. Diet is far more difficult, and yet far, far more important.

### Diet

*About three months ago I gave up eating wheat products, and if you look in your cabinet everything you have that is pre-packaged has wheat in it. The reason why is I was always feeling lethargic. Since then my cholesterol has dropped, my allergies have left, my waist size is down two inches, just for giving up wheat! I still eat the ice cream! ...Nobody told me that, I had to kind of figure it out for myself.[5] – Fox News host Bill O'Reilly*

I used to believe that fitness was about 50/50 diet and exercise, that they were equally important and that you could overcome a bad diet with lots of exercise. As it turned out, this is couldn't be more untrue.

My father was the biggest fitness nut I had ever known. A normal day for him involved a 15 mile run and some weight lifting as well. Marathons and triathlons were his passion. Healthy eating, however, was not. He used to say he could eat whatever he wanted because of how much he exercised. And at 41, when I was just 19 years old, he was dead – killed by a heart attack. His arteries were nearly 100% clogged by the fast-food heavy diet he lived on. The only reason he had not died much sooner was that his extremely powerful heart managed to still pump blood through the miniscule passages that remained open in his arteries. The additional exercise helped – it bought him some extra years on his life, perhaps as many as 10 or 15 additional years. But a healthy diet could have bought him many more.

### Lose the wheat, lose the weight

The evidence for this is becoming gradually more accepted in the health, fitness, and scientific communities, though the progress is uneven and sometimes agonizingly slow. While most workplaces generally recognize the danger of things like refined sugar, there is shockingly little awareness of the danger that *wheat* poses to your health and your career. In his book, *Wheat Belly: Lose the Wheat, Lose the Weight, and Find Your Path Back to Health*, Dr. William Davis recounts his gradual recognition of the damage that wheat was inflicting on his patients' health. His learning process started simply enough – many people don't know this, but wheat, *even whole grain wheat*, increases your blood sugar (i.e. it has a higher glycemic index) *more* than table sugar does.* So Davis started by advising his patients with high blood sugar to remove wheat from their diets. It worked, their blood sugars did indeed drop (as have mine since I eliminated wheat from my diet). But then other strange things started to happen too as they removed wheat. "They'd tell me all their joint pain was gone," Davis says, and more:[6]

> *Diabetics would become non-diabetic and came off their insulin and drugs. People with inflammatory and other immune diseases like rheumatoid arthritis saw dramatic relief and often complete cure. Acid reflux disappeared. Irritable bowel syndrome*

---

* I once worked with a diabetic whose doctor prescribed her whole grain wheat to treat her diabetes. I told her about the book and said that he may as well have prescribed her raw table sugar. Sadly, she didn't take me up on my recommendation to read the book.

*disappeared. Asthma, off all three inhalers. Migraine headaches gone for the first time in twenty years. Depression lifted. This went on and on and on.*

While gluten-free diets have become popular due to the many documented harmful effects of gluten (a protein found in wheat), gluten isn't the only culprit found in wheat and wheat-based products. Glyadin and AGEs, both found abundantly in wheat, are dangerous as well. They, respectively, stimulate addiction and make your body age faster than it otherwise would. Gluten or not, wheat is simply dangerous.

So what happened? Two things: the first, a theory posed by Davis, is that genetically modified "dwarf" wheat, a strain created in the 1970's to increase yields and combat world hunger, (unintentionally) made wheat dangerous to human health. The second is that beginning in the 1970's, just as the dangerous strain of dwarf wheat began to replace other, relatively harmless wheat strains worldwide, the U.S. government began pushing wheat as a key component of a healthy diet. The United States Department of Agriculture (USDA) to this day recommends that 60% of the human diet be composed of grains – a radical increase for many Americans and a completely unrealistic expectation of where most nutrients that humans need actually come from (mostly leafy greens and other fruits and vegetables). Meanwhile, the U.S. Surgeon General and doctors and dieticians nationwide latched onto a 1970's study that proved that *whole grain wheat was healthier than white flour wheat,* kind of like how filtered cigarettes are healthier than unfiltered cigarettes. But the medical profession went far beyond that conclusion – instead they made the conclusion, which still exists in the popular culture today, that this study proved instead that *whole grain wheat was actually healthy* period, full stop. Suddenly, just as wheat became dangerous to our health, doctors and dieticians around the country began to essentially offer prescription cigarettes as a treatment for lung cancer. Just when they should have been prescribing a diet free of (dwarf) wheat, our nation's experts began to tell you to eat more than ever. And then this happened:

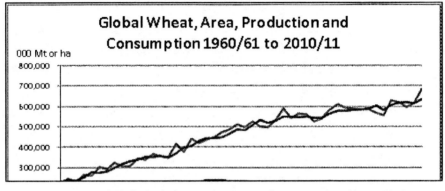

*Total global wheat production and consumption from 1960 to 2011. (Global area not displayed.) Grains Research & Development Corporation[7]*

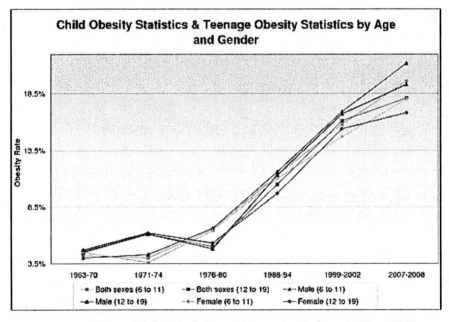

*Rising childhood obesity rates as shown from 1963 to 2008. Bariatric Surgery Source[8]*

Let food be thy medicine

The results have been a nightmare. Just as the U.S. began pushing increased consumption of "healthy" whole grains, American obesity exploded into epidemic proportions. The image of the "wheat belly," the effect where wheat fat accumulates in a person's belly and breasts, became so endemic that the popular portrait of the middle-aged American man went from the relatively slim, fit physiques embodied in shows like *Mad Men* to the rounded physique of Bob in Pixar's *The Incredibles*.

The effect on your work is far worse than even that image suggests, however. Some time ago I had a late afternoon meeting with a young intern. She started the meeting by complaining. "I'm so tired," she said. I was feeling very energetic myself, so I asked what she ate for breakfast. "I didn't eat breakfast," she said. Well, what did you have for lunch? I asked.

"A sandwich [with bread] and a Mountain Dew," she replied.

I told her that she was tired because of what she ate, and what she didn't eat. Basically, she did it to her herself, and it was ruining her work. Fortunately, the words sunk in, because about a year later after her internship had ended and she had taken another position, I saw her exercising in the office gym late after work. She was full of energy, had lost weight, and looked better than ever. When I asked her what had changed, she said it was mostly her diet.

The Greek scholar Hippocrates, founder of Western medicine, had a very strong opinion of the importance of diet to one's health. He believed diet to be the most important component of one's health, famously declaring, "Let food be thy medicine, and medicine be thy food." But modern American medicine, which supposedly stands on the shoulders of Hippocrates's theories (he is the author of the Hippocratic oath), sadly knows very little about diet, and as a result offers very poor – and often harmful, even deadly – advice.

Posture

Anything you do for hours every day has the potential to greatly damage your health, or at least your energy levels, if you do it wrong. Sitting is definitely one of them. If you sit improperly, you could damage your muscles, organs, spine, brain, shoulders, neck, and more! I've personally injured my own back and neck form poor posture *before I even turned thirty*. It can get very bad very quickly if you're not careful. One way to help with this is to sit in a nice, proper chair as much as possible. This is easier said than done – good work chairs run as high as $800, though you can find decent ones in the $200 range as well if you look hard enough (it's not easy). Any reasonable organization you work for will typically provide adequate seating, but not always, and be careful otherwise. In addition to appropriate furniture, simple improvements to your posture can go a long way as well, as this graphic by Bonnie Berkowitz and Patterson Clark of the *Washington Post* illustrates:[9]

# Don't just sit there!

We know sitting too much is bad, and most of us intuitively feel a little guilty after a long TV binge. But what exactly goes wrong in our bodies when we park ourselves for nearly eight hours per day, the average for a U.S. adult? Many things, say four experts, who detailed a chain of problems from head to toe.

REPORTING BY BONNIE BERKOWITZ; GRAPHIC BY PATTERSON CLARK

## ORGAN DAMAGE

### Heart disease

Muscles burn less fat and blood flows more sluggishly during a long sit, allowing fatty acids to more easily clog the heart. Prolonged sitting has been linked to high blood pressure and elevated cholesterol, and people with the most sedentary time are more than twice as likely to have cardiovascular disease than those with the least.

### Overproductive pancreas

The pancreas produces insulin, a hormone that carries glucose to cells for energy. But cells in idle muscles don't respond as readily to insulin, so the pancreas produces more and more, which can lead to diabetes and other diseases. A 2011 study found a decline in insulin response after just one day of prolonged sitting.

### Colon cancer

Studies have linked sitting to a greater risk for colon, breast and endometrial cancers. The reason is unclear, but one theory is that excess insulin encourages cell growth. Another is that regular movement boosts natural antioxidants that kill cell-damaging — and potentially cancer-causing — free radicals.

## MUSCLE DEGENERATION

### Mushy abs

When you stand, move or even sit up straight, abdominal muscles keep you upright. But when you slump in a chair, they go unused. Tight back muscles and wimpy abs form a posture-wrecking alliance that can exaggerate the spine's natural arch, a condition called hyperlordosis, or swayback.

### Tight hips

Flexible hips help keep you balanced, but chronic sitters so rarely extend the hip flexor muscles in front that they become short and tight, limiting range of motion and stride length. Studies have found that decreased hip mobility is a main reason elderly people tend to fall.

### Limp glutes

Sitting requires your glutes to do absolutely nothing, and they get used to it. Soft glutes hurt your stability, your ability to push off and your ability to maintain a powerful stride.

## LEG DISORDERS

### Poor circulation in legs

Sitting for long periods of time slows blood circulation, which causes fluid to pool in the legs. Problems range from swollen ankles and varicose veins to dangerous blood clots called deep vein thrombosis (DVT).

### Soft bones

Weight-bearing activities such as walking and running stimulate hip and lower-body bones to grow thicker, denser and stronger. Scientists partially attribute the recent surge in cases of osteoporosis to lack of activity.

**Mortality of sitting**

People who watched the most TV in an 8.5-year study had a 61 percent greater risk of dying than those who watched less than one hour per day.

| Hours of TV per day | Risk |
|---|---|
| 1-2 | 4% |
| 3-4 | 14% |
| 5-6 | 31% |
| 7+ | 61% |

## TROUBLE AT THE TOP

### Foggy brain

Moving muscles pump fresh blood and oxygen through the brain and trigger the release of all sorts of brain- and mood-enhancing chemicals. When we are sedentary for a long time, everything slows, including brain function.

### Strained neck

If most of your sitting occurs at a desk at work, craning your neck forward toward a keyboard or tilting your head to cradle a phone while typing can strain the cervical vertebrae and lead to permanent imbalances.

*Proper alignment of cervical vertebrae*

### Sore shoulders and back

The neck doesn't slouch alone. Slumping forward overextends the shoulder and back muscles as well, particularly the trapezius, which connects the neck and shoulders.

## BAD BACK

### Inflexible spine

Spines that don't move become inflexible and susceptible to damage in mundane activities, such as when you reach for a coffee cup or bend to tie a shoe. When we move around, soft disks between vertebrae expand and contract like sponges, soaking up fresh blood and nutrients. When we sit for a long time, disks are squeezed unevenly and lose spongIness. Collagen hardens around supporting tendons and ligaments.

### Disk damage

People who sit more are at greater risk for herniated lumbar disks. A muscle called the psoas travels through the abdominal cavity and, when it tightens, pulls the upper lumbar spine forward. Upper-body weight rests entirely on the ischeal tuberosity (sitting bones) instead of being distributed along the arch of the spine.

*Lumbar region bowed by excessive sitting*

### THE RIGHT WAY TO SIT

If you have to sit often, try to do it correctly. As Mom always said, "Sit up straight."

- Not leaning forward
- Shoulders relaxed
- Elbows bent 90 degrees
- Arms close to sides
- Lower back may be supported
- Feet flat on floor

## So what can we do? The experts recommend . . .

**Sitting on something wobbly** such as an exercise ball or even a backless stool to force your core muscles to work. Sit up straight and keep your feet flat on the floor in front of you so they support about a quarter of your weight.

**Stretching the hip** flexors for three minutes per side once a day, like this:

**Walking during commercials** when you're watching TV. Even a snail-like pace of 1 mph would burn twice the calories of sitting, and more vigorous exercise would be even better.

**Alternating between sitting and standing** at your work station. If you can't do that, stand up every half hour or so and walk.

**Trying yoga poses** — the cow pose and the cat — to improve extension and flexion in your back.

*Cow*

*Cat*

### The experts

Scientists interviewed for this report:

James A. Levine, inventor of the treadmill desk and director of Obesity Solutions at Mayo Clinic and Arizona State University.

Charles E. Matthews, National Cancer Institute investigator and author of several studies on sedentary behavior.

Jay Dicharry, director of the REP Biomechanics Lab in Bend, Ore., and author of "Anatomy for Runners."

Tal Amasay, biomechanist at Barry University's Department of Sport and Exercise Sciences.

Additional sources: "Amount of time spent in sedentary behaviors and cause-specific mortality in US adults," by Charles E. Matthews, et al, at the National Cancer Institute; "Sedentary behavior and cardiometabolic disease: A review of prospective studies," by Earl S. Ford and Carl J. Caspersen of the Centers for Disease Control and Prevention; Mayo Clinic.

*Illustration by the Washington Post's Bonnie Berkowitz and Patterson Clark*

# CHAPTER 9

# How can I save a lot of time?

*Nothing so needs reforming as other people's habits. – Mark Twain*

Multi-tasking is a lie.

One of the biggest lies floating around the modern workplace, in fact. Dave Crenshaw, in his essential Lynda.com training course *Time Management Fundamentals*, tells a story of a business owner he once worked with:[1]

> *She described a situation where she was doing three things at once: typing an email, talking to her assistant, and talking on the phone...She spent a total of one hour doing all three of these things at the same time...Well, finally she went out into the hall and took the phone call. To finish the call, it took her 7 minutes. She went back in to talk to her assistant. It took her 3 minutes. She sat down and answered the email. It took her 3 minutes. In short, when she tried to do all three things at the same time, it took her an hour and she accomplished none of them. But when she did them one at a time it took her less than 15 minutes, and she completed all of them successfully.*

You may still be a little skeptical, even after hearing that story. If so, please stop everything you are doing and do the following five-minute exercise.[2] Trust me, you will thank me. If you're feeling frisky, make someone else do it too. Their reaction will be its own reward:

1.  Take a piece of paper and a pen or pencil, as well as a timer (you can use your phone's stop watch app). You will time yourself doing two separate activities:

2.  First, time yourself doing the following: Alternate writing letters and numbers for the following two rows of words and numbers. Write one row directly above the other (i.e., first write "M" in row 1, then the number "1" in row 2, and so on until you finish both, as fast as you can).

*Row 1*

❖ <u>M y  C a r e e r  I s  T h e  M o s t  I m p o r t a n t
D e g r e e</u>

*Row 2*

❖ <u>1</u> <u>2</u> <u>3</u> 4 <u>5</u> 6 <u>7</u> <u>8</u> <u>9</u> <u>10</u>  <u>11</u> <u>12</u> <u>13</u>  <u>14</u> <u>15</u> <u>16</u>
<u>17</u>  <u>18</u> <u>19</u>  <u>20</u>  <u>21</u>  <u>22</u>  <u>23</u>  <u>24</u>  <u>25</u>  <u>26</u>  <u>27</u>  <u>28</u>  <u>29</u>
<u>30</u> <u>31</u>  <u>32</u>

3.  Second, time yourself completing this exercise one more time, but with one difference – do the entirety of Row 1 first before beginning Row 2. No alternating between letters and numbers this time. First all the letters, then all the numbers.

4.  Compare your times and how many errors you made.

Crenshaw calls multi-tasking by the name "switch-tasking." You can just think of it as "distraction." You will never perform your best work if you do not understand how to control distractions.

Crenshaw provides a number of very useful means to do so, but the most important one in my opinion is this: You must control your inbox. This is not necessarily your email inbox, but it can be. All information that you have must flow to one, or two or three, inboxes that you have, and you must be meticulous in managing it, cleaning it, organizing it, and enforcing its proper use. If you cannot control how you gather and maintain information – you have notifications pinging you every which way randomly, for example – and if you cannot limit the number of "inboxes" you have to no more than just one, two, or three, you cannot manage your tasks or your time. You will quickly lose yourself to switch-tasking and other distractions. For me, my "inbox" is my email inbox, and I spend time every day reviewing it, cleaning it, and improving its organization in some way. It is the backbone of my work, and I treat it with the care it requires.

### Tomato Techniques

When you have too much time to do something, your brain will often waste the time and use up all of the time you have available. Even if the task only takes 25 minutes, if you gave yourself two hours, then you will use the entire two hours. So when you have to get a task done, especially a simple task, instead of letting your lying brain waste your time, try instead to do it fast. If you really don't want to do it, try to do it *really* fast. **Race yourself.** Consider the Pomodoro Technique (the "Tomato Technique"), which has you break tasks down into 25 minutes each, with breaks in between. Making tasks smaller makes it easier to focus, work faster, and produce better quality. Another technique I use when I really don't want to do a bunch of menial tasks is I will decide to produce a *system* to help solve the problem for me, using computer software or filing systems. If I have to do something I don't want to be bothered with, I might as well create a "system" that will do it extremely fast, forever, right? And then when I have to do it again, it will take only seconds. Using these techniques, you can save a surprising amount of time, and have more fun all the while.

### Your brain lies to you

> Our consciousness lags 80 milliseconds behind actual events. When you think an event occurs it has already happened.[3] – David Eagleman

Your brain is a lying piece-of-you-know-what, and if you knew that, you would trust it a lot less and as a result waste a lot less time than you do now. Consider the following diagram of the Flash Lag Effect.[4] Imagine for a moment that in the real world, there are two separate things – a flash (the small circle) and a moving object (the large circle). In reality, for a split second, they are actually in the same exact position. But your brain, that lying piece-of-you-know-what, says they aren't *really* in the same spot, they're in two different spots! Some brain.

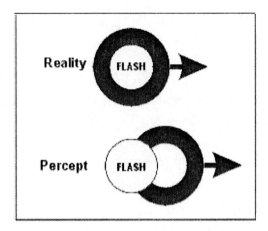

*What your brain sees vs. what reality sees:*
*The Flash Lag Effect[5]*

Oh, but it gets worse. Try this exercise developed by neuroscientist David Eagleman:[6]

> *Put this book down and go look in a mirror. Now move your eyes back and forth, so that you're looking at your left eye, then at your right eye, then at your left eye again. When your eyes shift from one position to the other, they take time to move and land on the other location. But here's the kicker: you never see your eyes move.*

Small potatoes, you might be thinking. But wait, it gets even worse! Research by psychologist Henry L. Roediger III has shown that your brain does even worse tricks to your memory. Say you have two memories – for example, two different items you need to buy at the grocery – and you're trying to remember both items. Well, when you cue up one of the two memories, your brain immediately starts to forget the second memory, to the point that, for many memories of yours, your brain will actually *replace* the second memory with the first one and forget it entirely.[7] In other words, the more you cue up memory #1, *the worse memory #2 tends to get.*

Ever have someone absolutely swear that you told them something that you never said? My wife does it to me all the time. Don't be mad at them, it wasn't wholly their fault, it was their *brain* (that you-know-what) that created that false memory. Your brain will actually, quite frequently, create memories of things that *never even happened*. For example, psychologists have found that if you give people a list of words – Thread, Pin, Eye, Sewing, Sharp, Point, Prick, Thimble, Haystack, Torn, Hurt, Injection, Syringe, Cloth, Knitting – and then ask them to recall those same words, they will often *swear* that they heard a related word (like Needle) that you actually never gave them at all.[8] Similarly, our brains tend to construct embellishments, or even entirely false stories of our pasts, based on this effect and others. One of those other effects is called Social Contagion – which is the process whereby someone else's memories (that you heard on the radio, on TV, or read on the internet...) become your own.[9] That brain, isn't it something?

No wonder then that in the courtroom eyewitness testimony has proven to be so unreliable that courts are now beginning to place restrictions on it.[10] As the New Jersey Supreme Court has discovered, our brains are "easily confused by similar situations and faces," which makes it quite easy for someone to falsely identify an innocent person as guilty.[11] Given what we know about the brain now, it's amazing that you-know-what was ever given the exalted status it had at all.

Of course, there's still more. Your brain will also distort memories depending on your emotional reactions, often for good reasons (to enhance your odds of survival), though of course at the expense of fidelity. When you're scared, time appears to pass slowly. Expect to recall those details well. When you're doing something new, your brain reacts more strongly than it would have had it been repetitive; expect it to recall "first time" experiences in greater detail than second time experiences, and so on. Boring events feel very slow in person, but are over very quickly when we recall them in our minds – our brain doesn't bother to store much information about them. The opposite is true of events that are exciting – for as much as time flies when you're having fun, your memory will conversely slow down when you recall it in reverie.[12]

### Don't trust your memory

Despite all of this knowledge that our memories are not to be trusted, people still try to, with terrible consequences. In *The Checklist Manifesto*, surgeon and public health researcher Dr. Atul Gawande describes how the increasing complexity in the medical field, and the strain this puts on the all-too-fallible memories of medical professionals, is driving horrific medical errors:[13]

> *Training in most [medical] fields is longer and more intense than ever. People spend years of sixty-, seventy-, eighty-hour weeks building their base of knowledge and experience before going out into practice on their own—whether they are doctors or professors or lawyers or engineers. They have sought to perfect themselves. It is not clear how we could produce substantially more expertise than we already have. Yet our failures remain frequent. They persist despite remarkable individual ability… Knowledge has both saved us and burdened us.*

Successful people like Dr. Gawande master their limitations not by shunning them, but by developing mechanisms to compensate for the biological limitations of the human brain – in Dr. Gawande's example, by mastering the use of checklists. Simple checklists! A completely-ordinary-mundane-*paper* checklist, as Dr. Gawande attests, has the power to turn around even the most dreadful hospital. To the 1970's philosophers that inspired his checklist manifesto, Samuel Gorowitz and Alasdair MacIntyre, this concept is known as "necessary fallibility" – there are things we wish to do that will always be out of our control. We must work *within* our necessary, simple, stupid, you-know-what fallibility if we are to succeed.

There are of course many examples where you will need to use your faulty, lying memory. The good news is there are a lot of techniques (that very few people use) that can radically improve your memory. I used these techniques to get into Harvard, for example. I describe these techniques in great detail in the chapter on going (back) to school.

In the real world however, in the vast majority of imaginable professional settings, you're much better off using a simple checklist like Dr. Gawande than trusting your faulty memory, even if your memory does use the fancy memory techniques I describe later in the book. Career success is about *making sure you don't get your job wrong*; it is not a game about who can memorize the most facts. Memory techniques take a lot more time to build then writing a "to do" list on a piece of paper, and success is as much about being efficient with your time as it is anything else. If a piece of paper is the most efficient and trustworthy option you have, then by golly use that piece of paper!

### The 8-Hour Workday

Another reason people struggle with time is they simply spend too much of it in one day on a given task. As the best basketball coach in NBA history, Phil Jackson, wrote in his book *Eleven Rings*, "If it can't be done in 8 hours, it can't be done." We far too often assume that if we just put in enough hours, maybe even sleep a little less, we can do better quality work. Yet there is no evidence to support that going beyond 8 hours in any given day on any given task will actually produce better quality work – yet there is a mountain of evidence that symptoms associated with long hours, like fatigue, are actively harmful. Carmaker Henry Ford is said to have discovered from internal research that the 40-hour workweek created maximum productivity. He is said to have noticed that while going beyond 40 hours could create initially short bursts in productivity, after a few weeks overall productivity would decline. Thus came to be the 40-hour workweek.

Even on your best days, you will typically only have 4, *maybe* 6, hours of highly productive work in you. The remaining hours in your day will be needed for rest, breaks, meals, transportation, learning, socializing, and various logistics. The key to saving time is to *maximize* those 4-6 hours of highly productive work you have in you. Don't blow it on a long lunch if you know you have a very important deliverable and a sensitive deadline. Knock it out during your most productive hours. Once you start having to use your *least productive* hours to do your most challenging work, you will likely find yourself working twice as long for half the quality – an ideal recipe for wasted time.

# CHAPTER 10

# How do I write a great resume?

*I'm not a very good writer, but I'm an excellent rewriter. – Pulitzer Prize-winning novelist James Michener*

Before you can learn how to write a resume, you need to learn how to write. Consider the story of New Dorp High School, which had once been one of the worst performing schools in the country.

Located in Staten Island, New York, New Dorp is a large, public school that for years struggled with poor student performance. The school tried everything, from firing bad teachers, introducing flashy education technology, to starting after-school programs. Nothing worked. Then, New Dorp instituted a new emphasis on – nay, a *zeal* for – writing. New Dorp began teaching analytic writing every day in nearly every class. The results were incredible: students who received the new instruction in writing were scoring higher on their tests than any previous class at the school. Pass rates for global history rose from 64 to 75 percent. For English Regents, the scores raised even higher, from 67 to 89 percent. Students had to repeat fewer courses. And best of all, they were getting closer to college: students enrolled in college-level courses rose from just 148 in 2006 to 412 five years later.[1]

The New Dorp principal responsible for these reforms, Deirdre DeAngelis, and her faculty had discovered that students were failing in large part because they could not translate thoughts into coherent, well-argued sentences, paragraphs, and essays, which meant they could not clearly think through and retain the information they were expected to learn. DeAngelis could tell which students were likely to fail simply by evaluating their ability to express their thoughts on a piece of paper.

### Writing well

You don't have to be a great writer – not if it's not in your Center, anyway – but you have to be a proficient one. Statistically speaking, there is a good chance you aren't. But we can change that, right now, with just a few basic concepts.

The first essential principal is *simplicity*. The hallmark of terrible writing is that it is difficult to understand; good writing never is. If you're not considered an expert writer (and even if you are, in many cases), do without flourishes and any unnecessary verbiage. The preeminent expert in this field, William Zinsser, writes, "Clutter is the disease of American writing. We are a society strangling in unnecessary words, circular constructions, pompous frills and meaningless jargon…the secret of good writing is to strip every sentence to its cleanest components."[2]

The second essential principal is *biggest point first, smallest point last*. Unless you're writing a movie with an incredible ending, nobody wants to wait to understand what it is you're trying to say – just say it first then explain it further as needed. In journalism this is known as an "inverted pyramid" – if you are writing a news story, the most important point goes first, into your headline. The second most important goes next, which is the story's introductory paragraph, and so on until the end. Getting this wrong is called "burying the lede." The next time you read a news article pay attention to this structure and see what you can learn from it.

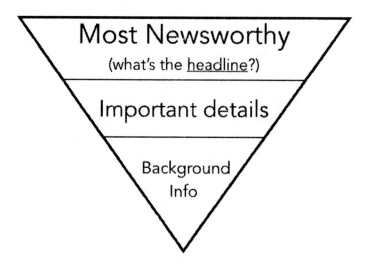

*Journalism's "Inverted Pyramid,"*
*a great general rule for communications.*[3]

The third essential principal is what Zinsser calls the *transaction*:[4]

> *Ultimately the product that any writer has to sell is not the subject being written about, but who he or she is...What holds me is the enthusiasm of the writer for his field. How was he drawn into it?*

For expanded reading, I highly recommend Zinsser's book *On Writing Well*.

## Communication

Let's try an exercise. You are a student at Beverly Hills High School and you work for the high school newspaper. Your journalism teacher gives you an assignment: write the front page headline for the following event:

> *Kenneth L. Peters, the principal of Beverly Hills High School, announced today that the entire high school faculty will travel to Sacramento next Thursday for a colloquium in new teaching methods. Among the speakers will be anthropologist Margaret Mead, college president Dr. Robert Maynard Hutchins, and California governor Edmund 'Pat' Brown.*[5]

What's the headline?

This was a real life assignment handed to Nora Ephron, star screenwriter of hit movies *When Harry Met Sally* and *Sleepless in Seattle*, on her first day of journalism class:[6]

> *She and most of the other students produced leads that reordered the facts and condensed them into a single sentence: 'Governor Pat Brown, Margaret Mead, and Robert Maynard Hutchins will address the Beverly Hills High School faculty Thursday in Sacramento . . . blah, blah, blah.'*

*The teacher collected the leads and scanned them rapidly. Then he laid them aside and paused for a moment. Finally, he said, "The lead to the story is 'There will be no school next Thursday."*

### The rules of writing

As important as writing is, sometimes you have to know when to break the rules of writing in the service of its higher purpose – communication. Communication is not just what you say but also how and when you say it, writing is just one answer to the "how" question. Understanding essential principles of communication can help you determine when to break the mold – like when to use that template someone gave you, and when to not use it and create your own instead.

The best book on communication you can read today is Chip and Dan Heath's *Made to Stick: Why Some Ideas Survive and Others Die*, which argues that ideas have a certain level of "stickiness" that determines whether they live or die. The Heath brothers have determined that successful ideas work when they are communicated in a way that is:

❖ <u>S</u>imple. Get to the point.

❖ <u>U</u>nexpected. Surprise them with a question, a fact, or a figure that challenges their assumptions.

❖ <u>C</u>oncrete. Provide real examples. Concrete is memorable.

❖ <u>C</u>redible. Be consistent, logical, and refer to authorities as appropriate.

❖ <u>E</u>motional. Why should they care?

❖ <u>S</u>tories. Story telling just works.

(Acronym: <u>SUCCES</u>)

If you bring those components to your communication, which includes your resume writing, you will be much more, *ahem*, <u>SUCCES</u>sful.

## Linking

One of the best training courses on writing that I ever took taught a concept they called "linking." The idea is that the word in each sentence should "link" to the first word in the very next sentence. This creates a very logical flow. So for example, in your resume, if you want to list three accomplishments and then want to explain one of those in greater detail, your biggest accomplishment should go *last* in the first sentence, and then it should *begin* the very next sentence. It is a subtle difference but it can vastly improve one's writing, especially technical writing.

## Resume writing

Resumes are one of the most important things you will write in your career, because they help get you into it, and they help you advance it. Resumes are critical for making an impression with your hiring manager; for opening up new mid-career opportunities for you; and for presenting your strengths and communicating your skills for awards and other opportunities. Your resume is in essence your first work assignment for your new job. Your resume represents who you are.

Here are some key tips to keep in mind when writing resumes:[7]

1. **Be organized**. Gather and compile all necessary materials and information, awards and previous resumes. Keeping everything in one place will make it easier to find accurate information and save time. Consider using a cloud service like Dropbox.

2. **Pay attention to key words**. Clearly articulate how your skills and experiences align to the information in the vacancy announcement. Keywords are action verbs. When explaining your previous experience, use action verbs as descriptions, expressing the action's performance and result.

3. **Be concise**. You are likely not the only person applying for a particular position. This means most resumes will get a quick glance, so you should only include information that directly relates to the position you're applying for.

4. **Highlight your capabilities**. It is crucial that your resume effectively sells your credentials. Key selling points need to be displayed at the top of the first page of the resume. Re-organize the format of your entire resume to do so if necessary.

5. **Use an editor's eye**. It's important to realize that a resume doesn't have to contain every detail of your past work experience. On the other hand, if you're applying for your first job and it requires writing experience, including your experience on the high school newspaper could be important.

6. **Use numbers to highlight accomplishments**. If you were a recruiter looking at a resume, which entry would impress you more? "Wrote news releases," or instead, "Wrote *25 news releases* in a three-week period under daily deadlines."

7. **Think time**. Organizations are always looking to save time and improve efficiency. Consider the appeal of the following resume line: "Proposed procedures that decreased average order-processing time from ten minutes to five."

8. **Follow the STAR Method.**

In your resume, you should clearly display your skills and the impact you have made in your previous jobs. The STAR method allows you to do just that. With the STAR (Situation, Task, Action, Results) method, you can create statements that highlight your past experiences and achievements while demonstrating your on-the-job impact. STAR statements focus on how you made a difference in your workplace and fill in the gaps in information about what you have to offer. STAR statements are much more effective at providing information about your contributions than a simple list of your duties.

Here's how to apply the STAR method in your resume to explain how you handled a challenging situation or task:

| | |
|---|---|
| Situation | Write about a specific situation in your work that presented a challenge to you. Provide precise details including who you were working with, what the challenge was, and where you were working so the hiring manager has a complete picture. You should also include information about your roles and responsibilities. Be careful not to overwhelm the reader with details — you don't want them to get lost or lose interest in your story. |
| Task you were given | Explain your role in the situation. What goal were you working toward? What were your duties? This part of the STAR method helps the hiring manager understand your specific role in the challenge. |
| Action | Explain the actions you took to solve the problem. What special skills or knowledge did you bring to the situation? How did you use them? Remember, your resume should describe the actions *you* took, not the actions of your supervisor or your team. |
| Result | Include a description of the direct results of your actions. How did your actions help to resolve the situation? Did you save the organization money? Did you improve a process? How many clients or customers benefited from what you did? Use numbers whenever possible to quantify your results and make your impact clearer to hiring managers. |

The following is an example of a resume entry using the STAR method:

*I inherited a complicated and confusing client referral system that delayed representative response times by two weeks. My task was to improve representative response times. I designed and implemented a new client referral system including data analytics, automated responses, estimated wait times, and easier access to basic information. I decreased client response time from two weeks to three business days. These changes increased the percentage of satisfied clients from 39% to 82% in less than one year.*

Now, let's break the entry down into each of the SMART method components:

<u>S</u>ituation: Inherited a complicated and confusing client referral system that delayed representative response times by two weeks.

<u>T</u>ask: To improve representative response times.

<u>A</u>ction: Designed and implemented a new client referral system including data analytics, automated responses, estimated wait times, and easier access to basic information.

<u>R</u>esult: Decreased client response time from two weeks to three business days. These changes increased the percentage of satisfied clients from 39% to 82% in less than one year.

### Federal resumes

The U.S. federal government is the largest employer in the world. Knowing how to write resumes for these jobs is important to making these opportunities available to you.

Federal resumes are different from many other kinds in that they are first and foremost used by Human Resources staff to evaluate your qualifications and weed you out if you don't effectively convey that you are qualified for the job at hand. They are not used to catch someone's attention and land an interview in the same way that non-federal resumes are. As a result, they tend to be longer, as many as 3-10 pages longer, than non-federal resumes, which are typically 1-2 pages long. Federal resumes also have a very specific format, which you can learn about using the website listed in the footnote at the bottom of this page.[*]

### Sample Resumes

---

[*] URL: https://mycareeratva.va.gov/library/resumes/training-course-resume-preparation.

Next I've included two resumes that I have used, one was the resume I used to apply for my first full-time job I got, the second is one I used years later. I highly recommend that you not copy them – they don't represent who you are, and they were written for very specific audiences. But hopefully you can learn from them and improve on what I have done.

**Resume #1.** This was actually a four-page resume for a job that focused on writing/editing and administration that I applied while still in school. Since I had extensive experience in both fields, I used a format of resume known as a "functional" resume – where I segmented my experience not by chronology, but by the type of skill I wanted to convey. Consider this approach if you have acquired your best skills from diverse experiences, such as through student extracurricular activities.

**Resume #2.** This resume employs a standard chronological format. It's also four pages long, though I'm only showing the first page here. As my eye for design improved, I made sure to communicate that by improving the style of the resume, especially the header, which is much improved over Resume #1's. Since design had become very important to me in the intervening four years, I wanted my resume's style to reflect that part of me. Unlike this version of Resume #2, most versions of Resume #2 that I used did not put my education first. I would typically place it last since professional experience is usually more important than education, but here it is again at the top because I was using it to apply to an academic program and that required that I begin my resume with my education.

# ANDRE JOAQUIN CASTILLO

2136 Z St., Washington, DC 20000 • andre.castillo@email.com • Phone: 909-555-5555

## EDUCATION

**Johns Hopkins University**                               **Washington, DC**
**School of Advanced International Studies (SAIS)**            **May 2010**
**Master of Arts, International Relations, GPA 3.75**

- Concentrations: International Economics and Middle East Studies, specialization in Emerging Markets.
- Selected coursework: Financial Sector Development in Emerging Markets, States & Societies of MENA, US Foreign Policy in the Middle East, US Military and its History, Latin American Politics.
- Awards: Presidential Management Fellow, *SAIS Review*'s Best Book Review, Class of 2007 Fellowship, Nemir & Nada Kirdar Fellowship, Bradley Fellowship, Critical Language Scholarship.

**California State University, San Bernardino**            **San Bernardino, CA**
**Bachelor of Arts, Political Science, GPA 3.85**                 **June 2007**

- Achievements: Alumni Scholar, Student Ambassador, Model UN Head Delegate & 7x award winner, Model Arab League 4x award winner, 2x Debate award-winner, SIK Presidential Achievement Award.

## EXPERIENCE AT A GLANCE:    EDITING EXPERIENCE

- *The SAIS Observer*, Johns Hopkins University-SAIS        **Washington, D.C.**
  Co-Editor-in-Chief, Writer                        Spring-Fall 2009
- *The Middle East Blog*, Johns Hopkins University-SAIS       **Damascus, Syria**
  Co-Editor-in-Chief, Head Writer                 Spring-Fall 2009
- The Law Firm of Mohamed Al-Sharif     **Yemen/Oman/Saudi Arabia**
  Legal Research Assistant                    Spring-Summer 2008
- *The Global Knowledge Report*, C.S.U.S.B.        **San Bernardino, CA**
  Editor-in-Chief, Head Writer                   Spring-Fall 2006

### PUBLIC SPEAKING EXPERIENCE

- The Johns Hopkins University - SAIS             **Washington, DC**
  International Trade Theory Teaching Assistant      Aug. 2009-Current
- AMIDEAST – Yemen American Language Institute    **Sana'a, Yemen**
  English Language Instructor                 March-June 2008
- National Model United Nations         **New York, New York**
  Head Delegate of Academics, 7x award winner    2004, 2005, 2007

### ORGANIZATIONAL EXPERIENCE

- **Office of Representative John Campbell**         **Washington, D.C.**
  Capitol Hill Intern                       March 2010-Current
- **C.S.U.S.B. Office of Housing and Residential Life**  **San Bernardino, CA**
  Resident Assistant (R.A. of the Month, January 2006)  April 2005-June 2007
- **Students for International Knowledge, C.S.U.S.B.**   **San Bernardino, CA**
  President and Founder                      2006-2007

### RECENT PUBLICATIONS

- "Censoring a Love Story in Tehran," *The SAIS Review*, April 2010.
- "Terror and Corruption in Mexico," The Center for a Just Society, January 2010.
- "Why Yemen?" Poets and Policymakers.com, December 2009.

### ADDITIONAL INFORMATION

**Languages:** Arabic (proficient); Spanish (intermediate); Turkish (basic).
**Study abroad:** Syria, Oman, Yemen, Israel, Turkey.
**Travel:** UAE, Saudi Arabia, Lebanon, Jordan, Egypt, Morocco, Spain, Canada, Mexico and Panama.
**Seminars:** Econometrics, STATA, Excel, PowerPoint, Negotiations, Conflict Resolution, Visual Basic.
**Interests:** sports, creative writing, volunteer work, surfing, culture, history, working with kids.

# ANDRÉ JOAQUIN CASTILLO

Castillo.Andre.J@email.com • Phone: 202.555.5555

*An expert in learning and leading change.*

## EDUCATION

Johns Hopkins University School of Advanced International Studies (SAIS)      Washington, DC
Master of Arts, International Affairs      August 2010
ẟ GPA: 3.75
ẟ Concentrations in Middle East Studies and International Economics. Specialization in Emerging Markets.
ẟ Student activist/organizer for development projects abroad and an economics teaching assistant, writer, and organizer at home.
ẟ Awards: *SAIS Review*'s 2010 Best Book Review; Class of 2007, Bradley, and Kirdar Fellowships.

California State University, San Bernardino (CSUSB)      San Bernardino, CA
Bachelor of Arts, Political Science      June 2007
ẟ GPA: 3.85
ẟ Student activist/organizer for improved residential life, foreign affairs/cultural awareness, and greater student involvement, including Get Out the Vote (GOTV) efforts.
ẟ Achievements: Alumni Scholar, Student Ambassador, International Model United Nations Head Delegate and eight-time award winner, four-time regional Model Arab League award winner, and two-time collegiate debate award-winner.

## PROFESSIONAL EXPERIENCE

U.S. Department of Veterans Affairs      Washington, DC
Program Manager      Nov. 2011-Present
Writer/Editor      June 2010 to Nov. 2011
ẟ Received Public Service Recognition Award from the Deputy Secretary of the U.S. Department of Veterans Affairs and recognized as a Presidential Management Fellowship Success Story (URL: http://www.pmf.gov/success-stories/andre-castillo-2010-pmf.aspx).
ẟ Consistently lead large, diverse teams; turn around underperforming projects and programs; and complete highly- visible, complex projects within scope, schedule, budget, and policy – and above expectations.
ẟ Serve as Program Manager for a large-scale, award-winning, Federal web-based program, MyCareer@VA, that produces and delivers career development training to Federal employees and the general public. The program has received more than 7 million web page views and 1.5 million visits since its launch in 2010, and has been shown to statistically improve employee behavior and career mobility. I am responsible for the program's IT infrastructure, training products, design, functionality, communications, acquisitions, and contract execution. Also responsible for the entire ADDIE cycle (analysis, design, development, implementation, and evaluation) of the program's training products, which include 14 web-based and in-person training courses and 8 dynamic data-driven web applications.
ẟ Lead National communications and marketing campaigns received by millions of people. Oversee communications strategy and tactics, coordinate with stakeholders, edit articles for National dissemination via the web, produce highly-regarded web-based marketing videos, and develop new methods of engaging customers that have been proven to be statistically more effective than industry standards. Provide speeches, presentations, and demonstrations to, and respond to inquiries from, the general public and senior Federal officials.
ẟ Lead National evaluations and data analysis for complex projects to analyze return on investment, employee behavioral change, customer satisfaction, and program effectiveness. Conduct VA-wide audits to assess areas to leverage other VA resources for cost reduction and prevent duplication of effort.
ẟ Designed, programmed, and implemented an all-in-one, multi-functional web-based management system

## How do I write a cover letter?

Cover letters are sometimes required in job applications. Traditionally a cover letter was a separate typed document, but today cover letters are often simply the body of the email that you send to an employer with your resume attached. Other than that, not much has changed. A typical cover letter is still brief and composed of just three paragraphs. The first paragraph is typically two to three sentences that state the name of the position you want to be considered for and why. The second paragraph is typically three to five sentences that convey what value you think you would bring to the job; it's very similar to your Elevator Pitch that is described in the chapter on how to ace your interview, refer to that section for more advice on how to write that paragraph. The final paragraph is often just one to two sentences that express your gratitude and answer any specific questions the job announcement requires (such as location or salary requirements). A good cover letter will overall serve five main purposes for the employer:

- ❖ *Convey your interest* (passion). Your first paragraph will state this directly, but it should also come across in the tone of the second paragraph.

- ❖ *Convey your skills* (strengths). The cover letter will explain how you will help their organization. Don't go into too much detail, your resume is best for that, focus instead on your overall story. I recommend you re-use your elevator pitch and tailor it accordingly.

- ❖ *Display good writing* (strengths). Basic skill in writing is expected in many jobs, and your cover letter will be evaluated on this. Refer to the book *On Writing Well* to learn more, which is covered in the chapter on resume writing. Mostly, be ready to revise, revise, revise.

- ❖ *Convey something interesting about you.* In writing your cover letter, you should also try and incorporate something about you that makes you sound like more than just a piece of paper. Since your goal is to get an interview, your cover letter should make you seem like someone the hiring manager wants to actually meet. A great example would be to reference an experience of yours that may help explain your interest or skills for the job. Think of volunteer, family, travel, or work experiences of yours and see if you can weave one into your second paragraph. Make it relevant to the job.

❖ *Answer the question.* If the employer asks for information, like location or salary requirements, don't forget to include it. If you don't, you run the risk of having your application ignored entirely.

## Sample Cover Letter for a Bank Teller position[8]

December 1, 2015

Joe Montana
49ers Bank Association
San Francisco, CA

Dear Mr. Montana:

I would like to present my application for the position of Bank Teller in response to your advertisement at the University of San Francisco, where I am currently finishing my Bachelor of Accounting. I believe my skills would make me a great fit for the position.

During my degree program, I have taken on a variety of work assignments, including internships and part-time jobs, where I have developed skills relevant to banking, finance, and customer service. I have a proven track record of professionalism, efficiently resolving customer questions and concerns, improving work processes, and providing accurate and ethical management of all transactions in my area of responsibility. In addition, my volunteer experience as head treasurer for our local chapter of *Meals on Wheels* has taught me the impact that sound accounting practices and good customer service can have on the community, an attitude which I would bring every day to this position.

Please find my resume attached. I would be very interested in meeting with you to discuss the position. I can be reached at (555) 555-5555. Thank you for your time.

Best Regards,
Jerry Rice

# CHAPTER 11

# How do I ace my interview?

*To speak and to speak well are two things. A fool may talk, but a wise man speaks. – English playwright and poet Ben Jonson*

Two words: *research* and *practice*.*

Interviewing is a form of public speaking. As with all forms of public speaking, the best preparation you can do is to record and watch yourself practicing.† Before you start practicing however, you should understand some basics about the following five types of interviews:[1]

1.  *Individual.* An individual interview is like an in-depth, one-on-one conversation. These and panel interviews often include performance based questions, also known as behavioral interview questions. The interviewer may be the person who will be your supervisor, so hiring decisions are often made based on this type of interview. You can count on discussing your skills, experience, and training, and how they all relate to the duties and opportunities of the job.

2.  *Panel.* A panel interview is frequently used by government agencies when filling a professional or managerial position. Usually three or more people sit on the panel/selection board, and all candidates are asked the same questions. This type of interview usually involves more structured questions than an individual interview. You'll need to be prepared to answer questions from several people. And remember, much like an individual interview, you will probably see several questions about your performance or behaviors. We will discuss how to prepare for those questions later in this chapter.

3.  *Virtual.* Virtual interviews are increasingly common, though I would never recommend choosing one over an in-person interview if you have the option, since it is harder to communicate virtually than it is in person. Of course, virtual interviews are typically conducted via phone or webcam. For webcam interviews, your background and posture are

---

* You like that beating I'm giving you, Mr. Dead Horse?
† The company InterviewStream provides excellent interview recording and practice services if you are interested.

extremely important. Make sure to dress appropriately, maintain proper posture and sit in a room without any distractions behind you. Wear business appropriate pants (you may have to stand up, and some interviewers even ask you to), and don't forget to lock out that cat! It is important to prepare for a virtual interview as much as you would for an in-person interview. Remember, as soon as you pick up the phone or turn on your webcam, you are giving them a sense of who you are as an employee.

4. *Stress.* Stress interviews are used by specialized organizations, such as law enforcement, to evaluate candidates. I went through a similar experience when training to become a Resident Assistant at my local university. Here, the interviewer's job is to intimidate you. The goal is to find out how you handle stress. The rationale behind the tactic is that if you're unable or unwilling to handle conditions of imposed stress, it's unlikely you'll have the ability to maintain your composure under conditions of real stress.

5. *Observational.* The observational interview format may be used for certain positions. The candidate is asked to demonstrate his or her abilities with some of the skills required for the position. This may include giving a demonstration of public speaking ability, answering telephone calls, or operating a piece of equipment while the interviewer observes your performance.

There are four stages to every interview. Your performance is evaluated at every stage:

❖ *Stage 1: Introduction.* In this stage, the interviewer forms an initial impression based on your greeting, appearance, and initial comments that can contribute to their hiring decision. Your goal of course is to make a great first impression. Smile, and introduce yourself with enthusiasm and confidence! The cliché is true – you never get a second chance to make a first impression. If any nice thoughts are coming to your mind (I'm grateful for the opportunity! What a nice office! I love your tie!), say them here. Just don't force it, it should be natural and truthful.

❖ *Stage 2: Employer questions.* In this stage, the interviewer's goal is to try and determine how well your skills and experience fit with the office's needs and culture. The interviewer is trying to match your specific skills and abilities to the job. Your goal is to answer the interviewer's questions with targeted, well thought-out (in other words, rehearsed!) responses that illustrate how well your knowledge, skills and abilities fit the office's needs. Adequately researching the position ahead of time and anticipating potential questions is key.

❖ *Stage 3: Applicant questions.* In this stage, the interviewer's goal is to determine your level of interest in the job and your degree of knowledge about the organization. This is the time to clear up any uncertainties. Your goal is to be enthusiastic and show your interviewer just how much you already know about the organization, and that you have clearly thought through how you would add value. Come prepared with specific questions to ask, but also ask questions relevant to what you have learned so far in the interview.

❖ *Stage 4: Closing stage.* In this stage, the interviewer will draw the session to a close. Your goal, if you are sure you want the job, is to make your intentions clear at this time. Remember, this is most likely your last chance to leave a good impression in person.

### Preparing for a successful interview

*Step 1: Be prepared.*

Anticipate questions and practice answers. Research the organization and the position, and save this information to your smart phone so you can refresh your memory before the interview or refer to it when it is time for you to ask questions. Prepare your questions for your interviewer in advance. Take a test trip to the location if you can. Know the interviewers' names. Get a good night's sleep and feel as good as you can physically beforehand. Bring all requested documents.

*Step 2: Look Good.*

Go to the interview neat and clean. Dress conservatively and comfortably. When in doubt, avoid heavy makeup and trendy or flashy clothes or jewelry.

*Step 3: Be Punctual.*

Give yourself enough time to get ready carefully. Leave your home with plenty of time to spare. Arrive at least 15 minutes ahead of schedule, but don't let your interviewer know you have arrived until closer to 5 minutes ahead of schedule, as you don't want to interrupt them. I once had a person I was interviewing arrive 30 minutes ahead of schedule and expect me to start the interview then. I was busy with another assignment and we did not have a waiting area, so I had to kindly direct her to the office building's coffee shop until it was time for her interview. Use the extra time to review the questions you will be asking, or to look up additional information about the organization.

*Step 4: Be Aware of Body Language.*

Silence your electronic devices. Offer a firm handshake. Stand or sit up straight but comfortably. Sit down only after offered a chair. Lean forward in your chair and relax. Don't fidget. Use eye contact but don't stare.

*Step 5: Carry a Portfolio.*

Show the interviewer that you planned ahead. Bring all necessary information: a pad and pen, samples of work (if appropriate; when in doubt bring samples that can support your answers to their interview questions), a calendar, your notes on the organization and the position, your questions to ask the interviewer, several copies of your resume, any correspondence from the application process, a copy of application documents, a reference list, letters of recommendation (if requested), and any other requested identification or documents.

*Step 6: Be Enthusiastic.*

Have a positive attitude in the interview. Be friendly, but not casual. Be professional and courteous to everyone. Don't be negative about anything. Sell yourself – the difference between bragging and self-confidence is enthusiasm. Use eye contact and voice expression to your benefit. Smile as you would in any conversation.

*Step 7: Say Thank You.*

At the end of the interview, thank the interviewer for their time. Follow-up with a brief thank you note that reviews points brought up in the interview and adds ideas you forgot to mention.

### Answering performance based interview questions

The best predictor of future performance is past performance, which is why *performance based questions*, or behavioral questions, are used during interviews. These questions require applicants to describe specific experiences that showcase their skills. The *STAR (Situation-Task-Action-Result) Method* will help you structure your answers appropriately. While the STAR method is ideal for answering performance based questions, it works for other question types as well.

**Situation.** Begin by describing the situation that you were in. Think about a specific event or situation, and avoid generalized descriptions. This situation can be from a previous job, from a volunteer experience, or any relevant event. Just make sure to give enough detail for the interviewer to understand.

**Task.** What did you need to do? What goal were you working toward?

**Action.** Describe the actions you took to address the situation with an appropriate amount of detail. What specific steps did you take? What was your particular contribution? Be careful not to focus on what the team or group did when talking about a project. Keep the focus on YOU. Use the word "I," not "we" when describing actions.

**Result.** Describe the outcome of your actions. Don't be shy about taking credit for your behavior. What happened? What did you accomplish? What was the impact? What did you learn? Make sure your answer contains multiple positive results.

Congratulations! You've completed your interview. Now it's time to sit back and wait for the phone to ring, right? Not so fast.

Remember, every interview is an opportunity to improve your interviewing skills. To help you learn from your experience and to maximize your chances for success, here are two things you should remember to do at the end of each interview:

- ❖ Follow-up by sending a thank you email or letter to the interviewer.

- ❖ Take a few notes about how you did. Written notes are best, but I often take mental notes as well, and just repeat them to myself several times until I have memorized them.

## Making your elevator pitch[2]

When you initially meet someone, his or her first impression of you is formed within the first two minutes. A well-crafted elevator pitch will help you make a first impression that is professional and memorable, which can help you land a job or expand your network.

### What is an elevator pitch?

An elevator pitch is a quick speech you memorize to use during interviews, networking events, and in case you ever meet someone who you need to make a good, professional impression on. An effective 30-second elevator pitch (about the time an elevator ride would take) can help you nab the career opportunities you're looking for.

The elevator pitch is your first big step in presenting your personal marketing proposition. It should help you stand out in an impressive and unique way related specifically to your career goals. That way, when the next big professional opportunity arises, you will be the first person that comes to mind.

The first step is to research and understand the opportunity you're looking for. For example, if you are looking for a particular job, memorize key skills required of that job and how your background fits into those. Remember, you are the product you are trying to sell – focus on the qualities and skills you have to offer, and tie them to the career that you are looking for.

The next step is to practice the six elements. Though they sound simple, becoming *great* at them will only come with practice:

❖ *Element 1: Greeting.* Include your first and last name.

  Hello, my name is ____.

❖ *Element 2: Experience.* Summarize your experience in your jobs and industry. Talk briefly about your major job functions and skill categories. If you are still in school, include any skills acquired through part-time, volunteer, or extra-curricular work if you think they are relevant and set you apart.

  I have ___ years of experience in the ___ industry with expertise in ___, ___, and ____.

❖ *Element 3: Strengths.* State specific skills that you possess. What would you most want the listener to remember about you?

My strengths are ___, ___, and ___.

❖ *Element 4: Accomplishments.* List a specific accomplishment or two that emphasize your strengths. These should allow the listener to understand how you would add value to their team. Examples can include an elite program you were admitted to or a significant project or change you created.

I have been recognized for ____.

❖ *Element 5: Professional Style.* Highlight traits that describe how you perform your job. If you are looking for a corporate or government job, you will probably want to emphasize speed, quality, and responsibility, and perhaps leadership as well.

I'm ___, ___, and ____.

❖ *Element 6: Job Goal.* What do you want to do? It can be a job or as simple as a new experience or opportunity to meet someone.

I'm interested in a career in _____.

A sample pitch:

> *Hi, my name is John Dover. My career has always been focused on government information technology. For the past five years I've been working for the Department of Defense on several IT projects, where I led teams charged with designing information security architectures. I've been recognized as a leader and innovator within my Department for implementing new methods to evaluate the performance of IT projects. Recently, I was awarded a Medal for Exceptional Civilian Service for completing a project that greatly improved the Department's local area*

*network in the Northeastern states. I'm always looking for Project Manager opportunities that will help me expand on my IT career.*

# Public speaking

To get the best out of your interviews, and the best out of your career, you should learn a bit about effective public speaking practices. You never know when it will come in handy, and it's much better to have the practice sooner rather than later. I entered public speaking competitions in high school and college, not because I expected to be great at it, but just so that I could learn, because I thought it would be useful. This paid off nicely one day early in my career when I was asked to speak for Federal News Radio. Our office's senior leader had originally suggested that I speak to this outlet, but due to a very short turnaround time I was not able to brief him with what I intended to say before I went on the air. When he found out afterward he gave me a friendly admonishment and recommended that I should have vetted my talking points through him first, which is of course great advice, and advice that I give to others as well. But then he listened to the interview.

After listening, he smiled, turned to me and said, "Have you done this before?" Why yes, I said, I had. Many times. Like with everything else, my advice is to get your practice in before your number is called. Opportunities come quickly and unexpectedly. In the information age, there is no reason why you can't already start preparing in advance for moments like these.

## Speech writing

*An effective...speech is defined not by rules of rhetoric, but by the character of response it evokes.*[3] *– Thomas Neal and Dana Ely*

To get started, I found this nicely done (and free) write-up by the Congressional Research Service that you can read freely online, created to advise Congressional speechwriters. According to its authors, Thomas Neal and Dana Ely:[4]

> Writing for the spoken word is a special discipline; it requires that...speechwriters' products be written primarily, although not exclusively, to be heard, not read. Speeches are better cast in simple, direct, and often short sentences that can be easily understood by listeners. Rhetorical devices such as repetition, variation, cadence, and balance are available to, and should be used by, the speechwriter.

As the report states, when writing any speech or presentation, practice isn't enough. It's also important for speechwriters to analyze audiences according to factors such as age; gender; culture; profession; size of audience; political affiliation, if any; and the occasion for, and purpose of, the speech. Most effective speeches do not exceed twenty minutes in length, and many are far shorter than even that. A few more tips that have helped me a great deal when I was a professional speechwriter:[5]

> Ideally, a speech draft ought to be reviewed three times: by the writer, by the prospective speaker, and by a disinterested third party. Of these three, priority should ordinarily be given to the speaker. The revised product is likely to be more effective. With speeches, as with food, however, too many cooks are undesirable. Moreover, time seldom permits this much critical evaluation and rewriting. It may even be easier to provide for some appraisal of the speech's impact and audience reaction after delivery. For example, it is said that Senator Robert F. Kennedy's speechwriters would follow his delivery of a speech word by word, noting those phrases or ideas that were well received, or others that created problems.

The "too many cooks" warning is also great advice. When I was a speechwriter, if a coworker offered advice on what I considered to be my area of responsibility – the prose and style of the speech – I would listen carefully and consider it, but I would not necessarily change my approach if I thought my approach was best. At first I would to try and please my coworker, but I quickly got out of that habit after I made a number of stylistic changes against my better judgment that the speaker later disapproved. Soon, I realized that only I was accountable for that element of the speech, so when in doubt, I would have to go with my own judgment. Otherwise, I wasn't doing my job.

## Negotiating

The 1995-96 Chicago Bulls hold the record for the best single season performance in NBA history, winning a record 72 games. That performance was far from expected: just the year before the Bulls had underachieved, losing in the playoffs to the upstart Orlando Magic spearheaded by a young Shaquille O'Neal. The Bulls' star player, Michael Jordan, was 32 years old entering the '95-96 season and was hearing serious doubts about his ability to compete for a title for the first time. When the Bulls' training camp kicked off before the season started, tensions were high. Jordan was more critical of his teammates than ever, to the point of causing friction between them. Steve Kerr, the Bulls' new 6'3" 175-pound three-point specialist, took exception one practice and began talking back to the much bigger, stronger Jordan. Jordan responded by driving into Kerr and hitting him with a forearm shiver to the chest. Kerr pushed back, and Jordan started throwing punches. Kerr responded in kind, and wound up with a black eye for his trouble. At the behest of the Bulls coach, Jordan called Kerr to apologize within the hour. The next day Kerr and Jordan talked it over and put it behind them.

According to then-coach Phil Jackson, this fight became a turning point for the team that went on to become the best in NBA history. After the fight, a mutual respect developed between Jordan and Kerr, and Jordan became a better teammate and leader. Looking back, Kerr says he did the right thing:[6]

*It was a totally different relationship from that point on. He became, I think, more compassionate to everybody, and definitely to me. He had a different approach than most people and he was such a maniac, the way he would kind of attack the game and the season, that he had to understand that everyone was different and not everyone was as talented as him and not everyone was made up the same way as him.*

Now, in most settings if you get into a fistfight with a coworker it will likely be the end of your job and perhaps your career. So don't do that, as sports are different, obviously, but this example illustrates how conflict, if done for the right purpose (as Kerr did in insisting he be treated with respect), can be a very healthy and potentially invaluable component of building a great career. "Knowing how to disagree agreeably with higher-ups," writes Joann Lublin of *The Wall Street Journal*, "increases your chances for advancement."[7] Even in office environments where physical altercations are (rightfully) banned, managers will welcome fact-based disagreement that is done respectfully, tactfully, and leads to good results.

### How to Argue with the Boss

So how do you disagree with higher-ups respectfully, tactfully, and in a way that leads to good results? You *negotiate*. And the best I've ever read on the subject of negotiating is Roger Fisher and William Ury's *Getting to Yes: Negotiating an Agreement Without Giving In*. Fisher and Ury offer five principles to follow in your negotiations:

❖ *Don't bargain over positions.* For Kerr and Jordan, they didn't bargain over Jordan's right to push his teammates and Kerr's right to not be berated, although both easily could have. They set those positions aside and talked instead about what was best for the team.

- ❖ *Separate the people from the problem.* Despite getting a black eye, Kerr didn't take the issue with Jordan personally, and neither did Jordan with Kerr.

- ❖ *Focus on interests, not positions.* Kerr, Jordan, and their coach focused on the mutual interest of winning games, which required being able to work respectfully and cohesively together.

- ❖ *Invent options for mutual gain.* Coach Phil Jackson made Jordan realize he could get better results from his team by apologizing and ceasing certain behavior, even though Kerr did not demand it. Even though it was a concession by Jordan, both Jordan and Kerr gained.

- ❖ *Insist on using objective criteria.* For Kerr and Jordan the objective criteria they used were respect and winning. They set those as most important (more important than who started the fight, for example) and used them to resolve the issue.

Now, if you get punched in the face, your best recourse is usually to call security (or the police), so don't think that negotiations are appropriate for *every* situation. But these principles are still highly useful in many situations in your career. They can be very difficult to implement in practice, especially if they go against your current habits, which for many of us they do. I highly recommend you obtain a copy of *Getting to Yes* to internalize the entirety of its lessons. My ability to negotiate has been absolutely essential to my career successes, as it has been for virtually every successful person you can probably imagine.

Your negotiations will begin from the time of your first interview – as soon as your prospective hiring manager begins to ask you about salary, benefits, or work preferences – and it will continue until your very last day on the job. How you negotiate your challenges, opportunities, and – as Phil Jackon's Bulls found out – your conflicts, will very often make the difference between a great achievement and a mediocre one.

# CHAPTER 12

# Should I network?
# Online?

*So we face a choice every moment of every day: We can fill one another's buckets, or we can dip from them. It's an important choice – One that profoundly influences our relationships, productivity, health, and happiness. – "Grandfather of positive psychology" Donald Clifton and Tom Rath*

In 1938, Harvard University initiated a study of 268 students. The researchers leading the study, later known as the Grant study, interviewed the individuals every few years to see how their lives and their careers would develop. At the time, researchers were most interested in studying men's physiognomy – did these men's "masculine" body types predict future success? Were those men who appeared more masculine more likely to achieve career and personal success?

As it turned out body type did not matter at all. But something else did. The men who grew up in homes with warm parents and loving relationships were more likely to reach higher ranks in the military, while the men who lived in colder homes were much more likely to remain as privates throughout the course of World War II. Body type was not the only useless predictor – social class, birth order, and political affiliation were each ineffective as well. No, a warm childhood trumped them all.

According to the director of the study, George Vaillant, "It was the capacity for intimate relationships that predicted flourishing in all aspects of these men's lives."[1] Some of the men in the Grant study who had weak relationships and inhibited emotional connections would initially experience career and marital unhappiness – even those highly educated men with degrees from Harvard – but would later turn their lives and careers around once they became more apt at recognizing and expressing their emotion.

Contrary to what you were likely taught, the core of professional networking is in building these emotional connections with others. Those who are able to do so effectively not only achieve better results in their own careers, they also build greater trust in others, thus creating a more powerful network that they can use to pursue new, more engaging career opportunities.

## Mapping your professional network[2]

Before you know how to improve your network, we need to get an idea of where your gaps are.

A helpful exercise can be to map out your current, indirect, and ideal professional connections. Current connections are people with whom you are already connected and have a solid and comfortable professional relationship with. These are people you know well and who you are likely in regular contact with. Indirect connections refer to people who you are connected with via a mutual connection. Ideal connections are people who you would like to have a professional connection with, but with whom you have not yet made any form of contact.

Sketch out the names of relevant direct contacts, indirect contacts, and ideal contacts on the following page:

## Your professional network map

## Expanding your network

Gone are the days when building professional relationships occurred mostly in person at conferences or events. In today's world, social media plays a huge role in helping us to maintain communication with people in our lives. In fact, online professional networking has now become part of how many of us do business. While it is important to expand your network to help you grow professionally, it is just as important to keep your current professional relationships strong. Starting and maintaining an online professional networking presence is a great way to begin this process. The following tips can help you to expand and enhance your online professional network while you work to strengthen your current relationships.

By expanding your list of contacts, you can benefit in several ways. You can connect with others who can mentor you through the career development process; have access to first-hand information about organizations and job opportunities; and have access to first-hand information about what the jobs you are interested in are really like. Use the following steps to expand your online network.

### Find past contacts

To expand your current network, start by thinking about the people with whom you have shared a lot of professional experiences – for example, you might remember former colleagues, past classmates, or people you met at a recent training session. Take a look at your contacts' current LinkedIn networks – they may be connected to other people you know in your field who you have not yet connected with online. Review your personal and professional email contacts and consider adding them to your network. Review the distribution lists of professional organizations or affinity groups you are a part of (for example, your school alumni groups, fraternities or sororities, professional associations, etc.) – reconnecting with people in these groups is a great option because you already have something in common with them. Review the connections you have made as part of professional associations or alumni groups, and reach out to the leadership of these groups.

Once you have found new people with whom you would like to network, email them or send an invitation to connect. Often, professional networking websites like LinkedIn generate a generic invitation message – consider personalizing the wording of this message to make it stand out from other invitations the connection has received (remember that your end goal is to connect on a personal level with your contact). When personalizing your message, make it easier for the contact to remember you by briefly mentioning how you know him or her, and if it applies, name the mutual acquaintance that introduced you. If you have only met once, consider also including a reminder of where and when you met.

### Leverage your current connections

Most people are eager to help their friends and coworkers connect. So using your current network to connect with new contacts is another excellent way to start new relationships. Often, your current connections can recommend others in your field and quickly put you in touch.

One way to approach someone in your current network is to email him or her and mention your area of interest (for example, Human Resources). Ask if your contact has any current or former coworkers who have experience in that field – most people will be happy to connect you if they know anyone in your area of interest. If you do not know the person well, it may be helpful to state how the two of you met and describe your current line of work. Sincerely thank the person in advance and be patient in waiting for a response.

If you have not heard back in about two weeks, feel free to send a follow-up email – in this message, politely state that you are following up on your initial email.

### Strengthen your current network

By strengthening your current network, you add value to your professional relationships. This makes it more likely that your contacts will ask for your opinion or advice; connect you with other individuals who can support your career development; or think of you when a career-related opportunity arises.

One of the key ways to make your professional network more meaningful is to stay in touch with the contacts in your network. Like all relationships, professional relationships need time and attention. When you stay in regular contact with your network and build solid business relationships, your contacts are likely to talk favorably about you to their colleagues and think of you when opportunities arise. Keep in touch with your connections by occasionally contacting them online or setting up in-person meetings.

Ask your contact for a brief update – what is the most exciting project that he or she is working on? How does your contact like his or her new position? What does his or her average workday look like? Explain that you are reaching out because you are looking for opportunities for development.

Ask your contact to share the most valuable career lessons he or she has learned – for example, your contact may be able to give you tips on your current career search or desired career path. Share some of your work-related areas of expertise as well as new interests you'd like to develop. Ask your contact if he or she knows of anyone else who might like to connect with you – the more you discuss your interests and experience, the more likely this will happen naturally and your contact will think of you in the future

### Continue to nurture your relationships

Although a lot of people are very willing to help build professional relationships, most do not enjoy being valued only for their connections. With this in mind, consider inviting your contact for a chat over coffee. This shows you care about nurturing your relationship and you appreciate your contact's time and assistance. Your goal should always be to build and improve your relationships with your contacts. Staying in touch is crucial to achieving this goal. In addition to exchanging emails occasionally, other methods for staying in touch include:

❖ Commenting on and liking the posts your connections make on social media. For example, if a contact posts a helpful article on hiring best practices, you might comment on what you found to be useful. Not only does this help to build your relationship with your contact, it also highlights your interests to others and helps you to build a connection online.

❖ Congratulating your connections as they take on new opportunities and gain achievements in their fields. LinkedIn will notify you of the changing roles or positions of your connections – whether you hear about a connection's achievements through social media, word of mouth, or directly, taking the time to notice and congratulate them will strengthen your relationship.

The steps outlined above will assist you in expanding and strengthening your network. Remember, however, that it is important to examine your connections often to determine whether you should take action to expand or strengthen your network.

### Effective communication and social networking

First impressions matter, especially when building professional relationships. When you contact a potential employer in person, by phone, or by email, your communication leaves an impression, so learning to communicate effectively is crucial. You should adapt your style of communication to fit an employer's expectations and leave them with a positive impression of you. How can you develop your communication skills to help guarantee a good first impression with a potential employer? Become familiar with these best practices.

## The employer perspective

Hiring managers are busy people, especially when they are trying to fill a position. They may be reviewing hundreds of applications and scheduling interviews, all while trying to complete their day-to-day responsibilities. Consider the employer's workload and use discretion when reaching out to them. Here are some tips to keep in mind when contacting a potential employer:

❖ Only contact potential employers when it is essential, like when you're scheduling an interview, confirming the receipt of documents, or sending a post-interview thank you note.

❖ Make sure your contact with the employer is polite, but direct, and that it includes all relevant information. Avoid constantly contacting the employer for updates — you do not want to overwhelm or annoy them. At the end of your interactions, ask about next steps and timeframes so you know when you will hear back and can follow up accordingly.

## Best practices for phone calls and emails

When contacting an employer by phone, keep these tips in mind to make sure you are professional at all times:

❖ Make calls in a quiet place without distractions, and if you are at home, make sure there are no loud noises in the background – no television, no noisy children, no barking dog. Introduce yourself and explain the reason you are calling. Be polite and direct. Respect the other person's time. If the contact person does not answer, leave one informative message that includes your name, your reason for calling, and your contact information.

For effective emailing with a potential future employer, use the following tips:

- ❖ Write a concise, descriptive subject line to immediately tell the reader the main point of your message. Use the contact person's name at the beginning of your message. Use correct grammar and punctuation (remember, your email is business correspondence). Do not use abbreviations or slang (for example, avoid shorthand like "u" in place of "you"). Avoid using all capital letters and extra formatting like bold, underlining, and italics.

- ❖ Carefully consider all of the information you need to include before sending the email, and try to include all of your questions in one message (this will eliminate the need for multiple follow-up emails).

- ❖ Keep your emails short and easy to read on a small screen as well as on a computer. Edit and reread your email to make corrections before you send. Make sure your tone of voice shows respect for the recipient. Sign your email using your full name and contact information to make it easy for the recipient to contact you in the future.

### Good practices for social networking

Social networking channels like LinkedIn, Facebook, and Twitter have changed the way we communicate. Different sites call for different styles and guidelines, so the way you write will often be determined by the channel you use. For example, Facebook is generally meant for personal and informal use, while LinkedIn is intended for professional use. Follow these guidelines when using social networking channels in professional situations.

Do:

Use LinkedIn to conduct basic research on the potential interviewer and organization to better understand their professional background before you speak with them. Join alumni and other affinity groups on LinkedIn to help you develop industry connections and improve your networking skills. Follow your target employer on Twitter to receive up-to-date information about the employer's accomplishments – consider mentioning these accomplishments in your interview. Check crowd-sourcing sites like Indeed and Glassdoor for an insider's perspective on jobs and organizations – you may even discover common interview questions used by your target employer. Make sure your Facebook privacy settings limit a potential employer's access to your private information, including photos and status updates (this allows you to keep your private postings private).

### Don't:

"Friend" professional contacts on Facebook or use Facebook to message them unless absolutely necessary – remember, Facebook is for personal use and blurring personal and professional lines can make you appear unprofessional. Don't post photos of yourself or your friends behaving inappropriately. Don't publish your opinions about work contacts or employers on Facebook. Don't complain or disparage current or past jobs or employers. And be very careful about posting opinions about political or controversial topics where your prospective employer can view them – this may put even your current job at risk.

### The 100 Coffees Challenge

In the chapter on how to get hired, I described how my friend Dan used the 100 Coffees Challenge to find his great job. The challenge goes like this:

- ❖ Set a goal to meet with 100 new people over coffee.

- ❖ At the end of each meeting, ask for the names of two additional people you should meet with.

- ❖ Don't ask outright for a job. Instead, ask for advice. Use your elevator pitch to explain who you are and what you have to offer. (Personally, my favorite question to ask is, "What is your secret to success?")

- ❖ Continue until you find the job you're looking for. Keep count of how many people you have met. Remain positive, and tell those who support you your running tally to keep the positivity going: "Off to have my 25th coffee today!" "Today is lucky coffee number 52!"

Think of a challenge that works for you. Maybe 100 coffees is too much for where you are in your career. At one point my challenge was to have drinks after work with a contact at least once per week. Before that my goal was to go to at least three conferences per year, and to make at least ten new, relevant contacts per conference. Later I modified that to be training and certification courses. The keys are to constantly be doing it, and to tailor it in a way that works for your goals and your industry.

### Informational Interviews

In one of the episodes of their famous podcast "Scriptnotes," established screenwriters John August and Craig Mazin receive a question from a woman whose dream is to move to Hollywood and become a screenwriter once her daughter graduates high school. She has one concern, however – she's deaf, and she's concerned that will affect her job prospects. She wants to know how she can learn more about what her best job prospects would be in the Hollywood screenwriting industry.

August and Mazin recommend a very valuable tool that you should consider using, especially when you have specialized needs or questions that are difficult to find answers to – informational interviews. An informational interview is simply a meeting where you ask a potential employer a few questions about working there. It can be in person (which is best), at their office or over coffee/lunch/drinks, or over the phone. Here are tips for having an effective informational interview:[3]

- ❖ *Identify the information you want.*

- ❖ *Act the part.*

- ❖ *Show interest.* A little flattery goes a long way. Say something like, "Mary gave me your name and told me you're considered to be an expert in your field. How did you get started?"

- ❖ *Have your elevator pitch, resume, and portfolio ready.*

- ❖ *Get names.*

- ❖ *Send thank you and follow up Letters.*

## The importance of flattery

In *How Full Is Your Bucket?*, Tom Rath and Donald Clifton examine the effects of negativity and positivity on employees. Negativity is not only harmful for business – one cited study found that *a single negative interaction* with an employee can scare off a customer permanently[4] – it is damaging for one's psychological and physical health. Rath and Clifton tell the story of Laura, who stays up all night to prepare for an important presentation. When she overhears a colleague whispering that Laura looked like she had stayed out all night – did she look that bad? she gasps – Laura loses her nerves, and her presentation falls apart. Research conducted by British scientist Dr. George Fieldman found that a negative boss can increase the risk of heart disease by a sixth and the risk of a stroke by a third.[5] Positivity, such as recognition and praise, on the other hand, has the opposite effect. This research led Rath and Clifton to develop the **Theory of the Dipper and the Bucket**:[6]

*Each of us has an invisible bucket. It is constantly emptied or filled, depending on what others say or do to us. When our bucket is full, we feel great. When it's empty, we feel awful.*

*Each of us also has an invisible dipper. When we use that dipper to fill other people's buckets — by saying or doing things to increase their positive emotions — we also fill our own bucket. But when we use that dipper to dip from others' buckets — by saying or doing things that decrease their positive emotions — we diminish ourselves.*

*Like the cup that runneth over, a full bucket gives us a positive outlook and renewed energy. Every drop in that bucket makes us stronger and more optimistic.*

*But an empty bucket poisons our outlook, saps our energy, and undermines our will. That's why every time someone dips from our bucket, it hurts us.*

*So we face a choice every moment of every day: We can fill one another's buckets, or we can dip from them. It's an important choice — one that profoundly influences our relationships, productivity, health, and happiness.*

Every day, you have a choice. You can meet someone, or greet someone, and you can fill the other person's bucket, or you can dip from it. The more you choose to fill it, the more your network will grow, and the more successful you will be.

## Seven steps for optimizing your LinkedIn presence[7]

LinkedIn is now the largest social media site with a business focus. In fact, two new members join the site every second. Additionally, LinkedIn is the top social media site for business executives – directors and above – and a recent survey shows that 92 percent of employers are currently using or plan to use social networks in their recruiting efforts. Here are seven steps you can take to truly optimize your LinkedIn profile and your network of connections:

### 1. Create a complete LinkedIn account

If you don't already have one, follow the step-by-step prompts on the LinkedIn website to set up a *complete* profile.

### 2. Maintain your LinkedIn account

Have you listed principal job responsibilities and duties under each of your work experiences? Make sure that this information is clear and precise – anyone who views your LinkedIn profile should come away with a solid understanding of your current and previous work experience.

### 3. Join and engage with professional organizations that interest you

Visit the websites and follow the media posts and blogs of companies, professional organizations or associations, and media outlets that interest you. Pay particular attention to the news feeds of your current company and other organizations you'd like to learn more about. This will help people viewing your profile better understand what you're interested in and whether you have any interests in common.

### 4. Regularly update your list of contacts

When you meet someone in your field, make it a habit to connect virtually with that person soon afterwards. The longer you wait, the more likely it is that you will forget about the acquaintance and miss the opportunity of connecting.

5. *Write or share posts*

Consider writing or posting articles about relevant topics that interest you. You can create original content or just "share" others' content, which easily increases the activity you display to others, which can help show your interest in the topic and highlight your desire for development. This matters to recruiters, and you never know who is paying attention. Just make sure you're sharing a good article – there's a lot of junk out there.

6. *Request recommendations*

Having another person's confirmation of your skillss can show others that your profile information is credible and accurate. Asking someone for a letter of recommendation to post on your profile is an excellent way to accomplish this.

When choosing someone to ask for a recommendation, think about people you've worked with most closely and who know you best. You want the person recommending you to have enough information to write a substantive letter. Current or past coworkers, supervisors, and fellow professionals are all possible options. Remember when asking a contact to write a recommendation for you that you should be prepared to return the favor if asked.

7. *Endorse others and seek endorsements*

The LinkedIn endorsement function is a less formal, simpler approach to getting a recommendation. It allows past colleagues to quickly and easily confirm or "endorse" that you possess a specific skill.

## Your online reputation

*#HasJustineLandedYet*

Justine Sacco had only about 200 Twitter followers. She was a Public Relations (PR) professional working for a PR firm that supported anti-AIDS initiatives in South Africa. A born South African, Justine was a passionate supporter of the plight of predominately black South Africans fighting insurmountable odds in Africa's AIDS epidemic.[8]

Just before boarding another long flight to Africa, frustrated at the ravaging death and first world callousness she perceived to be worsening this calamity, Justine sent a tweet that would live in infamy. Crucially, this flight would not have access to the internet.

> *Going to Africa. Hope I don't get AIDS. Just kidding. I'm white!*
>
> *— Justine Sacco (@JustineSacco) December 20, 2013*

Someone emailed Justine's tweet to Valleywag editor Sam Biddle, who tweeted it out three hours later.[9] On a typical day that would probably have been the end of it, but it was a slow Friday afternoon, and the day was just getting started.

> **Sam Biddle**  🖤 Follow
> @samfbiddle
>
> Very funny/cool AIDS/Africa joke from IAC's head of corporate communications, great work valleywag.gawker.com/and-now-a-funn...
>
> 1:30 PM - 20 Dec 2013
>
> **10** RETWEETS **14** FAVORITES

Members of the media began responding to Justine's account and the story gained traction. At first the response was mostly confusion. Why would Sacco, as a PR professional, tweet this offensive remark, and leave it up for so long? Normal twitter protocol would dictate a quick apology and deletion of the offending tweet. After all, famous comedian Steve Martin tweeted out an offensive tweet the same day as Justine, but the media moved on after he quickly apologized and removed the offending tweet.

But since she was on her (internet-less) flight to South Africa, Justine had no idea what was happening, and could not apologize or delete the tweet. Twitter users, unaware of this, saw the silence by Justine as obstinacy and became angry, and it had enough media attention that it wasn't long before the anger became a Twitter frenzy. *Twitterstorm* picked up the story, then *Business Insider* and *BuzzFeed*. Justine Sacco was now trending in Johannesburg, South Africa. Then, a woman in Miami created the hashtag #HasJustineLandedYet.

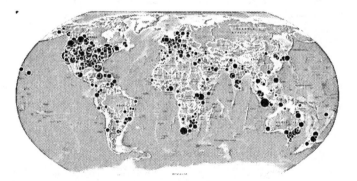

**Jim Forrest**
@todaysabacus                                                    🐦 Follow

Some stats on who's talking about #JustineSacco and #HasJustineLandedYet.  Hint, the whole world.

12:52 AM - 21 Dec 2013

**121** RETWEETS **67** FAVORITES

The hashtag was soon trending worldwide. The fact that Justine was unable to respond was now the story. The anticipation of Justine's response built dramatic tension for a news-starved worldwide audience. Famous personalities and companies began to respond. Photoshopped jokes spread. The non-profit AID for Africa, hoping to use the opportunity for good, purchased the domain www.justinesacco.com and redirected it to their fundraising page. The *New York Times*, CNN, ABC, and BBC all carried the story. The story had come to so much prominence that Justine Sacco's name was trending higher in search results than pop phenom Justin Bieber.

**jason**  
@Jason                                    🐦 Follow

Where were you when @JustineSacco landed? Second photo released, well done @reddit ! #HasJustineLandedYet

11:57 PM - 20 Dec 2013

**140** RETWEETS  **127** FAVORITES

When Justine landed just before midnight Eastern Time, she did not respond,* and instead deleted her entire Twitter, Facebook, and Instagram accounts. The next day, the final hammer fell. Justine's employer announced her departure from the company.[10]

### Lessons from Justine

Sacco was clearly the victim of bad luck. Reading her apology and history of fighting AIDS in Africa, the intention of her offensive statement was clearly, originally, a noble one – she wasn't

---

* She would later issue a heart-felt apology to local South African and international media outlets.

supporting the racial disparity of the AIDS crisis at all, she was *condemning* it. Because of her background and her good intentions, it's easy to see why she saw no apparent harm in making the statement in the first place.

On the other hand, there were clearly some unforced errors on Justine's part that contributed to the story and her losing her job. Let's examine those in greater detail.

First, Sacco clearly failed in her role as a Public Relations professional. Sacco's tweet was clearly offensive, well intended or not. Communications is not the study of intent – that belongs in the field of criminal justice – Communications is about impact, the *impact* that our words have on others. It's simply hard to read Sacco's message without cringing. As any communications professional should know, using a light-hearted tone to discuss a serious matter *generally* implies that you do not take that matter seriously, and *no one should ever take the impending deaths of millions of innocent people lightly*, which is exactly the message that Sacco implied. Once Sacco decided to become a PR professional, it then became her job to communicate that intent to us effectively, a job she failed to do in this instance.

This dichotomy between her professional role and the apparent offensiveness of her tweet is in fact what largely drove the story in its initial few hours. Just like how many feel a special motivation to publically shame a bad movie with a bad review on Rotten Tomatoes, or to shame an ineffective product with a poor review on Amazon, the general public feels greater motivation to criticize professionals because they are expected to produce a certain level of quality in their work. It's why we pay them! The mere thought of paying a professional for shoddy workmanship is often enough to make one apoplectic.

Second, in addition to displaying poor workmanship, Sacco underestimated the role that her online reputation played in her career. Reading her tweet, you get the sense that Sacco believes her Twitter account was not the same as, say, drafting an official company statement, that her Twitter account was instead a sort of space for her own thoughts. There is certainly some truth to that. Sacco's Twitter account is genuinely different than her day job – on her private Twitter account, Sacco can tweet about cooking recipes or share pictures of kittens for all she likes, acts she likely could *not* do in her daily PR job.

But your social media presence does share one thing in common with your day job – both convey to others who you are. Both Sacco's day job – drafting press releases, for example – as well as her Twitter account convey to others how good she is at her day job.

Imagine if you were a doctor who volunteered faulty medical advice on your Twitter account. If that faulty advice injured others, don't you think you would bear some responsibility? The general consensus, and the legal system agrees, that yes – your professional ethics do not end once you leave the office, and violating them can have consequences for your career.

Sacco decided to make a statement on her Twitter account that spoke, even tangentially, to her role as a PR professional, and when that statement did not measure up to the professional standards ascribed to her position, there were consequences.

### Delete, delete, delete

The final lesson to take from Justine is if and when you do make a mistake online, delete that mistake as soon as possible, and if you're truly in the wrong, you should apologize as well. Everyone makes mistakes and people are almost always willing to forgive them if you correct them soon enough. Giving the appearance of being a dilettante, on the other hand – intentionally or not – is a surefire way to provoke a backlash.

Now, don't think that just because you deleted it means it is gone. Many third-party websites back-up information automatically, whether they are offensive tweets or old web pages, so there's a good chance whatever you posted is saved somewhere forever. Still, the thought counts, and the likelihood that an employer will search deep enough to unearth anything a younger you may have posted and deleted is very low.

### Digital security

Matt Honen was expecting a call one Friday afternoon. He realized something was wrong when he went to plug his iPhone in and it suddenly rebooted to the setup screen. He entered his iCloud login to restore his information, but it strangely didn't accept it. Matt's iCloud account, and with it his laptop, Twitter, and email accounts had been taken over. Someone had been able to get a hold of his password and used it to take his Twitter account from him and wipe his laptop files clean, and with it Matt's irreplaceable photos of his baby daughter.[11]

Fortunately, Honen was able to recover his files, though it ended up costing him $1,690 for professional assistance. But it's easier than ever for malicious actors to cause you harm by obtaining your online information. Here are some easy ways you can protect yourself:

❖ Back-up all of your important digital information. I use Dropbox and gladly pay the $9.99/month for the space I need and happily recommend them, but Backblaze, iCloud, and Google Drive offer similar services as well that can take care of this for you. This won't just protect you against hackers deleting your files (assuming they don't hack into your cloud accounts too) but it will also protect you against inevitable hardware failure that will cause you to lose your data eventually, if you don't have a back up.

❖ Don't use the same password for multiple sensitive accounts, and don't use words or derivatives of words (i.e. don't use either "CareerTalk" or "C@r33rTa1k"), as both are extremely vulnerable to basic hacking techniques that anyone can learn in less than an hour.[†] Using Keychain or OnePassword can take care of this for you. (I use a mix of Apple's Keychain app as well as a spreadsheet saved on my iPhone, with iCloud disabled for the Numbers app; otherwise, if anyone hacks my iCloud account, they'll have access to the file that has all my passwords. This way the file is only on my iPhone – and wherever I back it up.)

❖ Consider investing in a service that will monitor your identity for you and notify you if it suspects any instance of identity theft. I use Identity Guard.

## New opportunities

For many people an online presence is a very low risk, low reward affair. You have a Facebook and LinkedIn account, maybe a Twitter and Snapchat account, but don't take any of them particularly seriously. But your online presence is quite the opposite – it is both high risk and high reward. High risk because almost everything you say is archived somewhere and can be dredged, and high reward because it can lead you to new opportunities. The web is unparalleled for the ease of access it provides to very smart, well-connected people across the globe, in addition to providing great training, learning, and business opportunities. If you use it wisely it can be your greatest asset.

---

[†] If you you're skeptical, you can read how one *Ars Technica* journalist taught himself how to crack your passwords: http://arstechnica.com/security/2013/03/how-i-became-a-password-cracker/

# CHAPTER 13

# Going (back) to school

*I've failed over and over and over again in my life. And that is why I succeed. – NBA Hall of Famer, five-time MVP, and six-time champion Michael Jordan*

The best free throw shooters in the NBA, like recently retired Steve Nash, have a unique habit. It looks kind of silly when you see it. Before they get the basketball to take their first free throw shot, they take a "practice" shot without the ball – nothing but air. An air shot. The idea is that this extra practice shot will help them in the seconds to come as they take their real shot.

The data bears this out. NBA shooters get better at shooting free throws the more free throws they have to shoot. NBA shooters shoot the worst percentage on their first free throw, then a bit higher on the second, and finally they shoot their highest percentage on their third consecutive free throws. In other words, if you want to boost your own free throw percentage, you should take a quick practice shot before shooting the real one. No wonder Steve Nash would take that funny looking air shot.

Now that I think about it – why does he take just one?

## How to get A's when you need them: *The Test-the-Test Method*

Like improving your free throw percentage, getting an "A" is easier than you think. How many times have you taken a test and thought to yourself, "If only I could take that test one more time! I would've done *so much better*..."? Getting an A is really that simple – just take the test again. And again, and again, until you get it right.

### Testing makes you smarter

> When students are tested, they are required to retrieve knowledge from memory...Various kinds of testing...encourage students to practice the valuable skill of retrieving and using knowledge. The fact of improved retention after a quiz — called the testing effect or the retrieval practice effect — makes the learning stronger and embeds it more securely in memory.[1] – Psychologist Henry L. Roediger III

I have been quintessentially a straight-A student my entire life, in every program I attended, from grade school through college and graduate school. My best performances, strangely enough, were actually in my most grueling classes, ones that were not only exceptionally difficult but also where I knew next to nothing about the subject material going into the class. (I'm thinking of you, Anatomy and Physiology and International Monetary Policy.)

My secret? I took the test in advance. Again and again, until my score was 100% (or close to it). That sounds like cheating doesn't it? That's because it (almost) is! It works so well, you'd think more people would do it.  Here's how you can too, using my *Test-the-Test* method. And not only will you not get expelled for it, you will actually be *applauded* for it. This method is not only how I received A's in my most difficult courses, it's also how I achieved extremely high scores on the LSAT and GRE that got me into Harvard Law and Johns Hopkins University.

### The *Test-the-Test* method

> [M]any studies reveal that much of what we learn is quickly forgotten. Thus a central challenge to learning is finding a way to stem forgetting.[2] – Henry L. Roediger III

First, before you can test-the-test, you need to have a test you can use. Sometimes, like when taking the LSAT or GRE, you can legitimately obtain copies of previous exams you can use to practice. If so, the next part becomes much easier and you can skip through much of it (though you should read it anyway).

If you don't have authorized access to previous exams, don't worry! You have an easy solution – you're going to create one.

### Creating the test

> The question is how to structure and use tests effectively... tests serve students best when they're integrated into the regular business of learning and the stakes are not make-or-break.[3] – Henry L. Roediger III

See that syllabus your teacher gave you? That's your key. Take it and look it over. See the different subject headings? See the titles of the assigned readings? Those will be your test questions that you will assign yourself.

So if Subject One of the syllabus is, "The Origins of the Ottoman Empire," then *question one* should be an essay question that reads: "Question One: What are the Origins of the Ottoman Empire?" If Subject One has four assigned readings under it, assign yourself four additional questions, one question for each assigned reading. Type each of these questions into a new, separate document on your computer. Format it so it looks more or less like a real test.

Next, go through your class notes. Do the same exercise for your notes that you did for the syllabus. Note any significant subjects or interesting facts that your teacher mentioned, *especially* if they weren't directly mentioned in the syllabus. Turn each of these significant items into a new question of their own, preferably an essay question (they're hardest and the best to practice with) or a fill in the blank question if that is more appropriate. Don't bother with creating multiple choice questions, it's not worth the time.

Now, your teacher may not be very interested in testing you on every single assigned reading or every topic that was covered in class. If so, great! Strike off those subjects that you think won't be on the test. Feel free to ask your teacher for advice on this as they usually (surprisingly) will advise you on what you should and should not study for. Just be careful – don't ever strike anything that might actually be on the test. If you do, you could be kissing your much needed "A" goodbye.

### Taking the Test

> *[T]he most common study strategies – like underlining, highlighting and rereading – create illusions of mastery but are largely wasted effort, because they do not involve practice in*

*accessing or applying what the students know.*[4] – *Henry L. Roediger III*

By the time you've finished this exercise you will have created one beast of a test. It may even be the hardest test you've ever taken. Good. Now sit down and take it, with no help. No open book, nothing, just like a real test. See how you fare.

If you're anything like me, you probably failed miserably. You might even have left some questions completely blank. And that's ok! You'll get another try. A lot more, actually. It's just good to know where you stand right away, as it will give you a good kick-in-the-rear if you're really behind but don't know it yet. It's better to fail now so you know to step up your study game sooner rather than later.

Next, look up the answers you need help with and write them into the test you took until you have what looks like a perfect "A" exam. Admire it, you deserve it. You just got an A on the hardest possible test you could take in that class. Now comes the important part.  See if you can take the test and get an A again, timed, but without any help.

Do this again and again until you have completed an A exam under realistic, test-like conditions. I would do this anywhere from a dozen to thirty times* before I would get the score I wanted. But once you've gotten an A on the *hardest possible test* your teacher could assign you, there's almost no *way* you're not getting an A on the real thing. This requires real work, but it's much more time

---

* For most courses I would only need 3-6 practices before getting an A, while the hardest courses required closer to a dozen practices or more. It was for the LSAT where I took upwards of 30 practice exams. The reason for that mostly that there is a much bigger difference in scoring a 95% vs. a 99% on the LSAT than there is on pretty much any other exam one might take. These small point differences determine the national law school rankings (bizarre when you think about it), so law schools take them extremely seriously. A 99% score versus a 95% score is essentially the difference between getting into Harvard Law and not, or getting a full tuition scholarship or no scholarship at all. (I scored a 172 the first time I took the LSAT and a 166 the second time.)

effective than you think. Maybe you don't need the A, but if you do, this is the method that will get it for you when you need it. I guarantee it.

## Your memory sucks – but you can make it better

Who's the smartest person you have ever met? What was it about them that made them seem so smart? For me, I've always been impressed when people can absorb and recite information. Their memories are so impressive! Those people must have what it takes to be successful, since being smart is the most important thing to being successful, right?

Wrong! As I grew older and met more and more successful people, one peculiar thing I noticed is that the successful people I knew were in many cases not quite as smart as many of the unsuccessful people I knew. I was meeting many people who had successful educational pedigrees, scholarships, fellowships, job offers, promotions, accomplishments, salaries, and I expected them to be the smartest people I had ever met. Sometimes they were, but the majority of them were actually what I would consider relatively average in terms of intelligence – at least, if you measure intelligence in terms of their ability to memorize information.

But what I have learned through my research and experience is that is actually exactly what makes them successful – they don't trust their own memories. *Not trusting their own memories* is what makes them take the precautions, like writing careful notes and double checking their assumptions, that prevent them from making catastrophic mistakes. This effect has been seen in schools as well. People who believe they are intelligent as a trait will perform worse on tests than those who are told that they are not intelligent, but that intelligence can be learned. Life Sciences, a health-science magnet school for predominately minority and low achieving students, tried splitting two groups of kids into separate 8-session workshops:[5]

*The control group was taught study skills, and the others got study skills and a special module on how intelligence is not innate. These students took turns reading aloud an essay on how the brain grows new neurons when challenged. They saw slides of the brain and acted out skits...After the module was concluded, Blackwell tracked her students' grades to see if it had any effect.*

*It didn't take long. The teachers—who hadn't known which students had been assigned to which workshop—could pick out the students who had been taught that intelligence can be developed. They improved their study habits and grades. In a single semester, Blackwell reversed the students' longtime trend of decreasing math grades....The only difference between the control group and the test group were two lessons, a total of 50 minutes spent teaching not math but a single idea: that the brain is a muscle. Giving it a harder workout makes you smarter. That alone improved their math scores.*

The Life Science children who performed worse were afraid to make mistakes and embarrass themselves, believing it would harm their image as the most intelligent students in the class. The students who were told they were not intelligent, meanwhile, had no such qualms and were able to take risks – risks that paid off by helping them make mistakes and learn faster, which ironically *made them more intelligent.* "When we praise children for their intelligence," Dweck wrote, "we tell them that this is the name of the game: Look smart, don't risk making mistakes."[6] Even if the result makes us all dumber.

Ed Cooke is well aware of this. Despite his own modest sense of his own memory – "I'm not a savant," he admits – Cooke is a recognized World Memory Championship competitor. He claims he has invented a code that enables him to convert any number from 999,999,999 to zero into a unique image that he can recall at any time in his mind. Cooke uses these images to memorize things like decks of cards and long strings of numbers against competitors from around the world. To keep track of all of these images, Cooke stores them in his memory palace – an entirely imaginary building in his mind.[7] The memory palace, a concept that can be traced back to the Greek poet Simonides and used to dramatic effect in the Benedict Cumberbatch television series hit *Sherlock*, is a technique that has you close your eyes and imagine a building. You then mentally "walk through" the building to remember its key facets. "Walking through" the imaginary layout aids your memory recall by using the relationships between the memories in your palace to help you find the memory you're looking for. Simonides used this technique to recount his survival from the tragic collapse of a Greek banquet hall. Competitors like Cooke use it today to memorize whatever facts and figures they desire.

Like the kids in Life Science, this technique has very little to do with any natural ability, but has very much to do with practice – it is simply the act of exercising your brain as a muscle. As Cooke himself states, "Photographic memory is a detestable myth, [it] doesn't exist. In fact, my memory is quite average. All of us [World Memory Championship competitors] have average memories."[8]

Personally I use the **memory palace** when I'm rehearsing a public event, like a presentation or a ceremony. In this method, you create a vision of a physical place and associate objects with it. You could think of a real location, like your home, and imagine the different Founding Fathers conducting various household chores. Then when it comes time for the quiz on who are the Founding Fathers, you could think back to your home and imagine yourself walking around the living room painted completely white and see James Madison escaping a fire, then walk into the basement and see George Washington constructing the foundation, then head to the bedroom safe where Alexander Hamilton is counting the money.

My favorite method for exams however is **note mapping**.[9] You can create outlines of materials in some visually ordered manner (1-2-3, ABC, etc.), using abbreviations to shorten it. It's a lot like writing a table of contents for a book, just make sure to squish it all on one page. *The key to creating a successful note map is to make sure you can make it all fit onto one page and you can memorize its visual layout.* What you're doing here is memorizing the layout of information like you would on a map. I would create note maps for final exams on very complex subjects, like science or law, and then re-create them the second the exam would start. This method is great at helping you to remember, for instance, that there are actually *three – not two!* – factors that fall under an element. So when the teacher asks me to "list each factor under that element," I know there are three (but not two) answers on my map, which helps me target my brain to finding them. If I've done a good job I'll have also memorized some kind of word or acronym from my note map for each factor as well that will trigger my memory for the whole answer.

A third method that you can use in conjunction with the above two is **word-image association**. Word associations I find are most helpful for lists, and associate an image (the more absurd the better) for the numbers one through ten and the words bun (for one) through hen (for ten). For example, *what are the 10 amendments of the U.S. Bill of Rights?* could be memorized as:

❖ Image: One, Bun. Answer: 1<sup>st</sup> amendment, freedom of speech. Image association: a loaf of bread is shouting into a microphone.

❖ Image: Two, Shoe. Answer: 2<sup>nd</sup> amendment, right to bear arms. Image association: A shoe with bullet holes in it.

❖ Image: Three, Tree. Answer: 3<sup>rd</sup> amendment, quartering of soldiers. Image association:    { fill in the blank }

And so on. What's the first amendment you ask me? Something to do with a loaf of bread shouting into a microphone, I think. Must be free speech!

The fourth and final technique I recommend[†] is the use of **acronyms**. If you must memorize a list of names, you could try rearranging the first initial of each person's name into an acronym. And if that acronym can form something close to a real word, or a whole sentence you'll find it even easier to recall later. If I told you WAJMM (pronounced "wuh-JAM") were the last initials of the first five U.S. presidents (Washington-Adams-Jefferson-Madison-Monroe), do you think you could remember that? One winner of a pi (the mathematical number with infinite digits) memorization competition won by breaking up pi into a series of marathon running times; he was a marathon runner.

You will not need these techniques to memorize everything, but they can help you memorize things that are quite complex. You should use them especially when you need to perform well in competitions, such as standardized tests. Techniques like these are how people have achieved great feats in memorization, and you may need them if you wish to achieve greatness as well. But remember, _no matter how good_ your memorization techniques are, they are _no_ substitute for simple on-the-job solutions like a paper checklist. Don't allow your hubris to lead you to overly trust your lying brain with memorizing complex information that can affect _people's lives_ when much simpler, more efficient, more effective solutions are available.

### Understand everything

Sometimes the challenge in front of you isn't memorizing a fact, it is understanding what that fact means at all. Especially if someone is telling it to you in person, like a classroom lecture, which is scientifically the most difficult way to learn. And while we love to talk, listening is incredibly draining. It's so easy to shut off and not understand what someone, especially a college professor, is telling us. We don't want to sound stupid, and we don't want to annoy them either. So often we just tune in and out, and maybe

---

[†] Mnemotechnics.org has even more strategies if you're interested.

even think of something else. But being a bad listener is no real solution at all either. Being a bad listener means you won't learn, it means people won't want to talk to you. And chances are, if you haven't had formal training and practice, that you're not a very good listener right now. Don't worry, we all were (I certainly was). We are born bad listeners. It's not in our DNA. Listening is a skill that has to be learned, despite what your parents may think. This is not an obvious concept, it wasn't until 1969 that an educational institution first recognized that listening was, contrary to popular opinion, non-passive, very complex, and a fundamental skill that required learning and instruction. I was fortunate enough to receive formal training in active listening while in college, and it has helped me in my career immensely.

For example, imagine the following scenario. You're sitting in a group. The people in the room are smart. Scary smart. And they're speaking in tongues. Or they may as well be, because you don't understand a word they are saying. Until, that is, you catch an idea that is similar to something you have heard before. Suddenly, subconsciously, you nod your head as if to say, "Yes, I get it now. I understand." The clouds begin to part as your brain whirs with that bit of daylight, and you pick up another idea that you understand, and another, and another, until you form a picture of what everyone else is jabbering about.

Then, someone turns to you and says, "Now, what do you think?" Just a moment ago, you would have been frozen in terror at the thought of answering any question at all. But now, you're excited.

"Well, I admit I'm not the expert on this," you say, "But I do have an opinion on three points – A, B, and C – that Mr. X and Ms. Y mentioned. And that opinion is...," you say, and go on to offer thoughtful insights. The conversation continues, and everyone leaves impressed with your small, but insightful contribution. And to think, just moments before, you had no clue as to what was happening.

This experience probably sounds familiar to you, because it's almost surely happened to you before. That's because this phenomenon is how you learn. It's how everyone learns. And understanding that is the key to understanding everything.

What happened to you in that experience is what education specialists call constructivist learning. Constructivist learning theory is an old but well-developed one, dating back to the dawn of the 20th-century and the work of philosopher-psychologist John Dewey. It argues that people learn by "constructing," or building, new knowledge on top of old knowledge. In other words, when people hear a new idea that is unfamiliar to them, they scan their brain for an old idea that is familiar and that can help to explain this new, foreign idea. If they are successful in that scan, then, as in the example above, they in effect nod their head yes, and add that new idea to their brain on top of the old one, as if it were a just a new story on their neural architecture of knowledge. If they are not successful in that scan, they become frustrated, perhaps even distrustful, and effectively tune out.

You've surely experienced both of these phenomena. The key to understanding everything is to get out of that cloud of frustration, and instead to figure out how to become better at building those new stories in your brain in the face of these confusing and complicated foreign ideas.

As described in the chapter on Strengths, learning is conducted by synapses, which transmit information and store them in neurons as knowledge for use later. As you age, your synapses get fewer but stronger, similar to how many floors add up to form a skyscraper. A child's brain, meanwhile, is like a vast array of townhouses.

The key to understanding everything and growing your neural civilization is understanding how everything connects to the ideas you already know and understand. It means cutting through the noise of newness and identifying that one familiar concept that you can latch onto, then using that familiar concept as a bridge to the other, new, foreign concepts, until they too become familiar. And so on, and so on, until, like in the example above, you leave understanding not every idea, but at least one, two, or three new ideas, to the point where you can very quickly repeat them and comment on them intelligently. Ignore the noise, focus on the familiar.

With this approach of building new ideas along with old ones, it shouldn't be long before you realize that everything around you is connected in some way. And once you do, understanding anything becomes merely an exercise in building those bridges within your brain. Since all languages are connected, there really is nothing actually preventing you from learning them all (other than interest and time, of course). Ditto for the sciences, technologies, and crafts. Or one of them, or two of them. Or three.

No, you won't be able to make a neural skyscraper of them all, just as you won't ever learn every single idea that comes up in every meeting you have with everyone. Your goals will need to be more realistic and practical – though this needn't lessen its significance or power in any way.

After all, what's a skyscraper without a view?

## How to get into Harvard

I took the SAT, California's primary college admission exam, when I was 16. I scored well enough that universities began to send me brochures in the mail, including Harvard University. I was stunned – Harvard was recruiting me? My GPA was very good and my SAT was good (but not great), so I thought I would have a good shot at getting in. I applied.

I didn't get in.

I would never forget how disappointed I felt that day. It was as if I realized something about myself was a lie. I really thought I was smart enough for Harvard, but this rejection said something else. I made it a personal mission of mine to figure out what went wrong. And then I applied again – this time to Harvard's law school, perhaps even more difficult to get into than their undergraduate program I applied to years earlier.

This time, I got into Harvard. This is how I did it, and you too can use the same method to get into the program that you think can lead you to greatness.

### Where I went wrong

The first thing I did was research what kind of people got into Harvard. Some of my research was online, but to the extent possible I met people in person and quizzed them about their experience and asked them for their advice. I learned that all university programs, including Harvard, generally care most about the following factors:

- ❖ Test scores.

- ❖ Grade Point Average (GPA).

- ❖ Extra-curriculars (your resume).

- ❖ Personal statement.

Letters of recommendation didn't hurt, but no one I could tell seemed to take them as seriously as the above four factors. The main lesson I took for letters of recommendation was to one, make sure you get them in on time! Even if it means pleasantly harassing your recommenders. And two, just get people who know you, don't worry about their titles. The admissions committee is really only using these letters to confirm what they think about you is true, so they need people who can actually describe you with a degree of accuracy.

I then gathered data on what the typical Harvard admittee had in the above four factors, mostly from Harvard's own website. I graded my own application to see how I would have done compared to your typical Harvard admittee:

- ❖ **Test scores: C-.** My SAT, while very good, was not nearly what a typical Harvard admittee had. This alone likely killed my chances. I learned that my mistake was not studying at all for the exam, had I had a serious study regimen I could have had a much higher score.

- ❖ **GPA: B.** My best grades came in my freshman and senior years of high school – years, I discovered, that counted the least to college admissions committees. My grades in my sophomore and junior years were equivalent to what a "C" quality applicant would have, while my freshman and senior years were an "A." I couldn't afford that hiccup again if I wanted to succeed.

- ❖ **Resume: F.** Again, my timing was off. I ended up finishing high school with very strong extra-curriculars, but they nearly all came my senior year. I transferred to a new high school my sophomore year and took too long to build up my resume. And even what I did accomplish, as my research showed me, was nothing compared to my competition. Here, my competition had blown me out of the water.

- ❖ **Personal Statement: B.** I had built up even at that age an above average skill for writing, so looking back I determined I was ok here. But I wasn't great, the other personal statements I was competing with were still better, I learned. I would have to step up my game here, and the trick I learned was revise, revise, revise. The greatest personal statements, like nearly all great work, go through many revisions to get there.

This was a "C-" application! No wonder I didn't get in.

Before I even decided what I was going to apply to for graduate school, I made sure that unlike in high school that I had no hiccups in my GPA or extra-curriculars, I hit the ground running freshman year and didn't let up until graduation. When it came time to apply again I decided to take a shot at Harvard Law. Researching their website I learned that the *average* admittee to Harvard Law had a college GPA around 3.8, a Law School Admission Test (LSAT) score of around 168, and, I assume very strong extra-curriculars and a great personal statement. (Yale Law actually does its applicants a great favor and sends a sample *great* personal statement along with the very advice I needed to be able to write one – revise, revise, revise!).

With extra-curriculars and GPA taken care of, I focused on getting myself to that "A" grade I needed on my LSAT and personal statement. For the LSAT, I aimed for a score of 170. For my personal statement, I aimed to create that feeling that great personal statements had – you couldn't stop reading, and in your heart you knew that the applicant who wrote the statement *cared enough* to be great.

When I finally took that LSAT, I scored a 172, which is in the 99.9[th] percentile of test takers, or about as high as you can score before the scores stop to matter. How did I do it?

First I researched, and then I used the *Test-the-Test* method.

I took the best instructional course that was around, which at the time was (and probably still is) TestMasters. They taught me the skills I needed to approach the test correctly.

After that, I took dozens of practice exams under realistic settings. At first my scores were relatively low, in the 150's. I checked to see what I got wrong, learned my lessons, and like a baseball player practicing his swing in the batting cages, I did mini practice exercises until I learned to do the problems the right way. And then I took more practice exams and repeated the process. Slowly my scores started coming up into the low 160's. Then the mid-160's. And then the high 160's. Until one day, I started scoring in the low 170's. And when that day happened, aside from a refresher exam here and there, I was done studying for the LSAT.

*Practice, practice, practice!*

Next came my personal statement. Like the Heath brothers say in *Made to Stick*, I knew I had to tell a story. Ultimately I settled on a story that I thought met two important criteria – first, it was interesting, a story I could tell to anyone on the street without boring them. Second, it explained something I really cared about. I settled on a story of a victim of war I had met in my travels who suffered brain damage and was no longer able to get the PhD he had planned for, and the wife and family he hoped would come with it. I made a connection between this story and my desire to prevent conflict, then shared it with two people – one a student, one a professor – whom I trusted to provide me with feedback I could use to *revise, revise, revise* it into a great piece of writing.

By the time I was done with my application, I gave my application an "A" rating across the board. Much better than the "C-" application I had submitted back in high school.

And it worked – I got into Harvard. Even though I declined the offer (it didn't fit into my Center as well as the schools I ultimately chose), it was one of the greatest feelings I have ever had. I'll never forget how I felt when I realized what I had believed about myself wasn't a lie after all – I *was* good enough for Harvard. I just needed to have the right mindset, and then put in the work.[‡]

And *you* are good enough too to be great at whatever is within *your* Center. Once you learn what that is, all you have to do next is put in the work.

### Harvard is overrated

I ended up not going to Harvard, as I didn't think it played to my strengths, opportunities, and passion as much as the other

---

[‡] See the chapter on "What if…" for an explanation of why the hours mattered as much as they did.

options I had. So I declined. Harvard is a great school and a great opportunity, but it's important to understand that it only accepts a very small percentage of people each year, and also that it can't teach *everything* – it is, by definition, not for everyone. And as Frank Bruni writes in his book, *Where You Go Is Not Who You'll Be*, you could go to school anywhere and still be very successful. To give just two examples that Bruni mentions, the CEO of Disney, Bob Iger, went to Ithaca College, and Howard Schultz, CEO of Starbucks, went to Northern Michigan. [10] And when the *Wall Street Journal* asked recruiters to name the five best universities for entry-level hires, do you know who they named? Penn State, Texas A&M, the University of Illinois, Purdue, and Arizona State – good schools, but all public, non-Ivy League universities.[11] These schools are similar to my undergraduate university, California State San Bernardino, where I was able to cut my teeth in their well developed leadership programs at a very young age – experience and training that has set me apart from my peers, and made me extremely *happy* and productive, ever since.

What school you go to matters, but only so far as it advances your Center – and that school can be anywhere. If it doesn't, you're not going to be nearly as happy, or effective, as you think.

## Law school: think twice

Law degrees are great if you want to be an attorney, you pretty much (with a few exceptions) have to have a J.D. to become one. But being an attorney isn't for everyone, and having a J.D. isn't nearly as empowering for non-attorneys as some would have you think.

J.D.'s are three-year programs that often cost around $150,000 just for the three-year's worth of school and living expenses – enough to buy a house. And that doesn't include the salary you're giving up by leaving the workforce. If you're giving up three full years of work at around $50,000 in annual salary, your J.D. program is now costing you a total of $300,000!

$300,000 is a lot of money. And you're not paying that back right away either – a typical starting salary for a full-time attorney is around $40-50,000 per year. Over time that can rise to a comfortable six-figure salary, so if you're willing to commit to the profession it will definitely pay off. But think long and hard before you do.

I actually spent one semester in law school and then left to pursue other opportunities I was more passionate about. I also didn't think the degree was worth my money or, most importantly, my time. Not that I didn't enjoy it. I loved learning what I did and meeting the people I met, a number of whom I consider life-long friends. But never once has any one of those friends said anything other than I made the right decision, and never once have I had any experience that indicated otherwise. A few years after departing law school I received this message through Facebook from one of those friends I met at law school:

> Andre, I just left law for a happier life. You having the courage to do it helped me realize it was a good thing.

This message warmed my heart that something I did had such a positive impact on the life of another person. But it also alarmed me – how many other people are making the same wrong choice that my friend made, and that I made as well?

If you're thinking about law school, think long and hard about it. Does the job you see yourself being happy in require a law degree? If it does, then law school was literally made for you. But if that job doesn't, don't you think you could be doing something more relevant than spending three years learning about apartment leases, court filing deadlines, and the legal reasons why Coca Cola doesn't ship most of its soda in glass bottles anymore? All of those things may be interesting to you, but will it help you with your career, and more importantly, help you to be happy?

Years later, I ended up returning to law school to get my degree because many years later I thought that yes, at that point in my life, being a lawyer would make me happy. I have since accomplished the goals I felt I needed to accomplish first – *create* (not litigate) things that helped others, travel more, get married, and start a family – and, importantly, this time I aimed for a law degree that I could afford. Instead of going to Harvard, I found another good school that would give me the scholarship and location I needed to make the decision make financial sense for me and my new family.[§]

## Master's degree: think thrice

Master's degrees (M.A.'s or M.S.'s) are probably of even more questionable value than J.D.'s. The reason is, unlike J.D.'s, a Master's degree doesn't typically qualify you for any particular position. It's like the person who graduated high school or college with more credits than you. It's nice to have, but someone with less education may actually be more qualified – if they have more *work* experience.

I actually have a Master's from one of the best master's programs in the world, and I am very glad I do, but it cost me. My master's program cost me $100,000 in expenses plus another $100,000 in approximate salary that I lost by not working during that time. For me, however, it was worth it – the M.A. qualified me for certain positions that I could not have obtained without it (a U.S. Presidential Management Fellowship), and which put me on track to make a significantly higher salary than I would have made without having a Master's degree. I did the math, and it worked for me.

Other Master's degrees where the math works out well include:[12]

---

[§] If you do decide to go to law school, I highly recommend Robert Miller's book *Law School Confidential: A Complete Guide to the Law School Experience.*

❖  Master's degrees that qualify you to be Physician's
   Assistant (P.A.), such as a Master's in Physician Assistant
   Studies (MPAS), Health Science (MHS), or Medical Science
   (MMSc). In many hospitals a P.A. is functionally equivalent
   to a doctor and often receive salaries in the six-figure
   range. The MPAS was ranked by *Forbes* as the best
   Master's degree to get in terms of job prospects.

❖  Master's Degree in Computer Science; Electrical
   Engineering; Mathematics; Information Systems; Physics; or
   Economics. The mid-career median salaries are each
   around six figures with high projected job growth for
   holders of those degrees.

❖  Master's degrees that your employer (or a scholarship)
   would pay for. Many employers would pay you, for
   example, to get a Master's in Business Administration
   (MBA), which can prepare you for a corporate management
   position. (MBA's are less useful for smaller businesses or
   new start-up companies. In those environments technical
   work experience is generally much more important. Keep
   this in mind if you want to start a business or don't want to
   work for a large corporation).

Other Master's degrees that pay well and have strong job
prospects include: Occupational Therapy ($79,200 mid-career
median salary); Health Care Administration ($87,800); and Nursing
($85,900). Everything else – *buyer, beware.*

## PhD: highest of its kind

If you asked yourself, "What does greatness in my field look
like?" you may have answered that it looks like someone who has
a PhD. PhD's are typically five-year commitments with a heavy
emphasis on researching, teaching, and writing in a highly
specialized field. If that sounds like a great life then a PhD is
probably for you.

Whereas an M.A. or J.D. is designed to communicate to the world that you hold a minimum level of proficiency, what a PhD tries to communicate to the world is that you are *among the most knowledgeable* experts in your field. In other words, you are someone to whom I can safely pay for expert advice, or someone that I should listen to on the radio or on television, or someone whose writing I should be reading online.

That sounds great, doesn't it? Who doesn't want to be paid for providing advice? The downside is to truly be *among the most knowledgeable in your field* is not easy, and often carries significant professional and ethical responsibility. It requires a certain lifestyle, a certain academic rigor and discipline to ensure that you have *read all there is to know* about your field and that you are providing sound advice accordingly. PhDs are expected to *at least be aware of* everything that their field has to offer in terms of knowledge. They are also often expected to contribute to that body of knowledge through their own research experiments and/or written publications. PhDs often teach or provide other consulting services in addition to their research responsibilities, and is how many PhD holders end up spending the majority of their working hours.

For advice on how get into and succeed within a PhD program, apply the same techniques I discussed earlier in staying within your Center, mapping your career, and "getting into Harvard." The only caveat I might add is that PhD programs are relatively more interested in research and writing than other programs, so you should be trying to get published as much as possible (with relatively unique research if you can) long before you ever submit your first PhD application, even if you are self-publishing or being published by publications no one has heard of. The practice and experience alone – remember, *revise, revise, revise!* – will provide you with a significant edge over your competition.

A PhD is setting you up to *be* someone – start *being* that person right now. See if you like it.

# CHAPTER 14

# What if...

*I know I'm not the best singer and I know I'm not the best dancer. But I'm not interested in that. – Madonna, 1991*

## What if I want to be an artist?

Madonna is one of the most successful entertainers in American history. Dubbed the "Queen of Pop" and "the most media-savvy American pop star since Bob Dylan"[1] by *Rolling Stone*, Madonna has sold tens of millions of albums in a career spanning four decades. *Forbes* estimates her net worth to be around half a billion dollars.[2] Madonna is a singer-dancer. For a singer-dancer to be this successful, you would think she was the best singer-dancer of her time. But she was far from it.

From early on in her career, Madonna displayed a remarkable capacity for self-awareness. "I know I'm not the best singer and I know I'm not the best dancer," Madonna admitted in 1991. "But I'm not interested in that.[3]" Instead, what Madonna was interested in – what she was passionate about – were the entertainment and business components of her career. It was her dedication to those parts of her career, she believes, that truly set her apart and led her to super stardom. Madonna knew her Center, saw that it set her apart and gave her a unique advantage, and she went for it.

Of course many, many hours of work also went into Madonna's rise to super stardom. In his book *Outliers*, Malcom Gladwell documents just how many hours widely successful musicians, from Mozart to the Beatles, had to accrue on their path to reaching career greatness. The magic number Gladwell discovered was 10,000 hours – Mozart and the Beatles needed just about 10,000 hours of practice in order to become truly great. Gladwell applies this number to greatness everywhere. Bill Gates? He had 10,000 of hours of practice too, and before anyone else could reach that number in his field (computer programming), which gave him the crucial edge over his peers that launched him on his path to billions.

Yet Gladwell has received significant criticism for his 10,000 hours theory. It's not hard to find exceptions to the 10,000 hour rule if you look for them. Many people *eventually* accrue 10,000 hours of work in a particular field without ever becoming great. So why does 10,000 hours work for some to achieve greatness and not others?

Gladwell himself admits that 10,000 hours is only an opportunity for greatness, not a guarantee. It wasn't merely that Madonna only put in the hours that made her so successful, *she was also relatively good* (strengths) at the business and entertainment side of pop music; *she was passionate* about it (try listening to that quote without hearing her passion come through); and, at the time, *she was the only female pop singer doing it* (opportunity). There weren't many people in the world that could say the same at that time. This was the beginning of Madonna's path to greatness.

Now, if you account for Madonna's Center, and acknowledge that people like Madonna, Mozart, and Bill Gates all had this factor in common – Gladwell's theory starts to make more sense. If you had an opportunity, if you had the talent, and if you had the passion, *and you then put in 10,000 hours of work – could you not also be great?*

The answer is *yes, you can*. And *that* is exactly what it takes.

That is where the true power of Gladwell's 10,000 hour theory lies. And if you want to be a great artist these same principles hold for you as they would anyone else. Only, the competition is likely to be greater – so you *better* put in the hours, and sooner rather than later, if you want to succeed.

### Flailing around

> I would say that there's truth to [comedians being "sad clowns"], but there's also a lot of sad clowns that are accountants. I worked in warehousing, there were a lot of sad clowns out there. There's a lot of people that, if you had a rough go of it as a kid, it doesn't always translate into you going into show business or the arts. I think that there's people on Wall Street that are compensating for whatever mountain is in your head when it's usually

*something you can step right over. That's something that I*
*continue to learn as an adult. A lot of my fears and anxieties are*
*the fears and anxieties of a six-year-old boy. When I finally*
*confront them, they're really small.*[4] *– Comedian Bill Burr*

Bill Burr is a successful comedian known for his stand-up specials, his hit *Monday Morning Podcast*, and various roles in *Breaking Bad* and *Chappelle's Show*. He had no idea he would one day get into comedy; instead, he started his career with various odd jobs. First he worked as a dental assistant before trying his hand in sales and warehousing. "You know what I was doing?" he recalls. "I was flailing. I was just trying everything because I wasn't good at anything. The only thing I was good at was f------ around, making people laugh."[5] Then one day Bill's friend says he's going to try stand-up because *hey, I'm funnier than those other guys, so why not?* Bill had never even considered getting into show business, but he hears his friend say this and thinks, "If he can try it, I can try it."

Unfortunately for Bill, opportunities to making a living in stand-up comedy were hard to come by in the 1990's when he first started. Stand-up comedy had had an economic boom in the 1980's and then just cratered, so there wasn't as much money to go around. But Bill knew that he loved it and was good at it, and besides, what else was he going to do? So kept with it:[6]

*I did the artist thing, I f------ ate spaghetti five nights out of the*
*week. You'd make the big f------thing of spaghetti with the Prego,*
*and I would shove, like, ten pieces of bread down my throat and*
*hope that filled me up for the rest of the day. I was big on that*
*and pancakes. Pancakes were another thing that just filled you up*
*for the day. It was like pouring concrete into your stomach. I f-----*
*- hate pancakes to this day. If you were on the road you went to*
*the Denny's or the IHOP, and you didn't get the short stack. You*
*got the five pancakes. Every time I would get three down and*
*when I got to the fourth one, I wanted to puke. I would just*
*shovel it down in there, just to fill up my stomach. I could go all*

*the way from the morning to the gig that night without eating. Hopefully at the gig that night they'd have some sort of bulls--- chicken fingers or mozzarella sticks you could just shove down your throat.*

Bill knew he had a long road to climb so he played it smart and was financially very conservative while starting out. He lived with his parents for the first three years and paid down his student debt while driving a "piece of s--- truck," as he puts it, so he could also save up just enough money ($5,000) to move to New York where he could make a run in one of the few scenes that had a strong economy for comedians. In the meantime, he lived in Boston, which also had a great stand-up scene, which allowed him to get the valuable training he needed. "I really feel like I got a priceless education when I was there [in Boston]," he recalls. "I was also able to get my timing down. When I went down to New York I got 40 minutes of material. I'm not gonna say it was good, but I had 40 minutes of material." When he got to New York, after about eight months he was able to make a full-time living from just stand-up.[7]

Looking back, he doesn't hesitate to say it was all worth it. Ask Bill what he thinks about his job now? *He (expletive) loves it.*

## What if I'm a woman? Or a member of a minority group?

Larry Summers is a world-renowned economist, and perhaps the most successful economist of his time. After earning his PhD from Harvard in 1983, at just 28 years of age he became one of the youngest tenured professors in Harvard's history. In 1991 he was tapped to lead the World Bank before ascending through the Clinton administration to ultimately head the Treasury Department in 1999. He would later serve as a key advisor to the Obama administration during its attempts to fight the Great Recession from 2009 to 2010. For at least two decades, if not longer, Larry

Summers could easily lay claim to being one of the smartest people in the world.

In between those two distinguished periods of his public service, Summers served a stint as president of Harvard University. As president of Harvard he delivered a speech addressing gender disparities in the fields of science, technology, engineering, and math. Far fewer women served in these fields than men, and he had an idea as to why. There were numerous studies showing that fewer women scored in the highest percentiles of scientific aptitude tests, he recounted, which meant fewer women who were able to fill these jobs. The main reason that women were not keeping up with men in these fields, Summers concluded, was that "there are issues of intrinsic aptitude."[8]

The reaction to Summers's remarks about the "intrinsic aptitude" of women was irascible, and the furor it caused led to his resignation the following year.

### The innate aptitude study

A team of researchers led by Sarah-Jane Leslie of Princeton University and Andrei Cimpian of the University of Illinois at Urbana-Champaign decided to study the question Summers had tried to answer – What is causing gender disparities in certain career fields?[9] Here, the study focused on academia. The researchers sent questionnaires to more than 1,800 American academics across 30 fields, ranging from astronomy to sociology. The questions were meant to test four competing explanations: was it longer working hours that kept women out of certain fields?; Was it that the discipline was very selective and difficult to get into?; Does the discipline emphasize thinking abstractly over thinking emotionally?; or, finally, is it that experts in the field think that you are born with an aptitude for that discipline (that are you born "good at science," for example)?

The first question came back negative, there was no correlation between female representation and hours worked.

Women were not less likely to be represented in an academic field because it required working longer hours.

The second question came back negative as well. The most selective of programs, the most difficult to get into, did not have less female representation. In fact, they had slightly higher female representation, though the difference was not statistically significant.

The third question, whether the career field emphasized abstract thinking over emotional thinking, also came back negative. It didn't make a difference in terms of whether women were more or less likely to be represented.

The fourth question was the only one to come back positive. If the experts in an academic field in University A's School believed that, to succeed, you had to be innately good at their discipline, you would have fewer women than you would at University B's School, *even if University B's school was the better, more selective school.*

This is how a social prejudice works. In this example, *University A's school is the weaker school.* If the explanation that men are innately at the higher end of the intellectual spectrum is correct, *the weaker school, University A's school, should have more female representation.* But that is not the case. Schools that emphasize merit over innate talent, *University B*, have *higher* female representation. It is only the schools that make women feel *unwelcome*, despite their credentials, by believing that (white) men have a higher "intrinsic aptitude" for these fields that in fact have statistically lower rates of female representation.

### Minority representation

The study found that it wasn't just women who were affected, African Americans were affected too. Like women, African Americans face the stereotype of lacking innate abilities for various academic disciplines, and this prejudice results in lower African American representation in schools like *University A's school.*

Schools that focused on hard work and merit were more likely to have African American representation in addition to higher rates of female representation. So everything I just said about women applies equally to minority groups as well.

### Strengths, talent, and hard work

In his book *Outliers*, Malcom Gladwell recounts a story of a woman named Renee trying to solve a math problem. In the video, Renee is using a software program to solve an algebra problem. On the screen is a graph with an x-axis and a y-axis. Her goal is to figure out how to draw a vertical line – a line with infinite slope. But it can't be done. In the videotape, Renee struggles with the program for twenty-two minutes until she discovers the truth, what Berkeley math professor Alan Schoenfeld, who made the video, calls a "glorious misconception."[10]

Renee is not a "natural" at math, but she solved the problem. It took her twenty-two minutes but she figured it out, and, importantly, she learned and remembered it. Most high school students, professor Schoenfeld recounts in *Outliers*, give up on a problem after just two minutes, which is not nearly enough time to actually learn the skill of math.[11] They assume that because they do not figure it out immediately that they have no innate ability for it. But that's not it at all – *they are just giving up too soon.* "Success," Gladwell explains, "is a function of persistence and doggedness and the willingness to work hard for twenty-two minutes to make sense of something that most people would give up on after thirty seconds."[12]

A study by Johns Hopkins University sociologist Karl Alexander supports this. In his study, Alexander studied the "achievement gap" between poor kids and wealthier kids in the city of Baltimore. Alexander compared the results of low, middle, and upper class elementary school kids on the California Achievement Test. Initially, the results showed that lower class kids were scoring *much* worse than upper class kids, which indicated a systemic failure of the public school system. However, Alexander discovered that those initial results were based on test scores that were administered after the end of a long summer vacation – in September. When Alexander looked at the test results from *before* summer vacation started, in June, there was no "achievement gap" between lower and upper income kids at all – *the test results were identical. The achievement gap was entirely caused by how the wealthier kids spent their summer vacations.*[13] During those summer vacations, the wealthiest kids' average reading scores shot up more than 52 points. The poorest kids' scores remained flat.

There is no identifiable innate ability that the wealthier kids possessed that the poorer kids did not. It was the simple time spent, the habituation of the doggedness required to push through to accomplish the work.

Innate strengths, or talent, are real, but it is unique to you and not based on your gender or ethnic background. Many people misunderstand their true strengths, particularly women and members of ethnic minority communities, because of social prejudices they have experienced in their lives. You should take care to not let social prejudice discourage you or those you mentor from developing their true strengths every day. You are not "inherently good at science," though you may have a talent for analysis or creative thinking, *either* of which may lead to success in science. Science, technology, engineering, math – these are not strengths; they are *skills* that you must develop.

Your strengths are the way you approach them. Not only do they have nothing to do with your gender or social or ethnic background, they also do not determine what career you can have. Two different people with two different strengths can work in the same career field. For example, one person's strength can be thinking about the past ("Context" as Gallup calls it), while another's can be thinking about the future ("Futuristic"). And they both can be pilots or lawyers, or doctors, or entrepreneurs. One who uses "Context" learns from successes and failures of the past, the other who uses "Futuristic" imagines new possibilities to take advantage of new technologies. Both approaches work.

If you have any doubts about what your true strengths are, you must invest in an in-depth assessment tool such as Gallup's StrengthsFinder to learn more about them. Once you know your true strengths, the remaining ingredient to your success then becomes simple hard work. If you do this, you can and will succeed regardless of your background.

Despite his world-renowned intellect, Summers was wrong, and it cost him his job. You do have unique talents, but they do not limit you to any one career field – it is only our own cognitive prejudices that do. You can be just as good a scientist or an engineer as anyone, if you are willing to work for it, and if you apply the strengths that make *you* unique to that career.

If you want to get the results to lead you there, such as a higher test score, as I describe in the *Test-the-Test* method in the chapter on going (back) to school, there are methods that you or anyone else can use to get them.

# CHAPTER 15

# Leadership

*Somewhere between the janitor and the CEO, reasons stop mattering. – Steve Jobs*

Steve Jobs was declared Fortune magazine's "CEO of the decade" for his role in leading Apple from near-bankruptcy to the world's most profitable company. Jobs liked to tell a story to his incoming Vice Presidents that captured his take on leadership. As Jobs would tell it, there was a janitor who is responsible for cleaning Jobs's office. One day, the janitor fails to empty his garbage bin; the garbage is still there. When Jobs asks why is the garbage still there, the janitor explains that the locks have changed and he doesn't have the new key. The janitor gives Jobs an excuse. To Jobs, this is acceptable. It is appropriate for a janitor to explain why he couldn't take out the garbage. "When you're the janitor," Jobs would tell his new VP, "reasons matter." But, "somewhere between the janitor and the CEO, reasons stop mattering," Jobs continued. "That Rubicon is crossed when you become a VP."[1]

Staying at the bottom of a career ladder, like a janitor, means being able to make excuses. Advancing your career into higher positions however – positions of leadership – means gradually relinquishing your ability to make excuses, and instead learning how to find solutions to problems that appear to be out of your control. And the sooner that you can demonstrate this ability, the better.

### Strengths based leadership

In their book *Strengths Based Leadership: Great Leaders, Teams, and Why People Follow*, Tom Rath and Barry Conchie tell the story of Sarah. Sarah has just had *a great week* at the office, when suddenly Sarah finds herself dreading going to work. She dreads it so much that she nearly feels ill. At first, Sarah doesn't know why.

After wracking her brain she finally figures it out – her boss, Bob, is returning to the office today from *yet another* training course on leadership. Sarah already knows what Bob is going to do. He's going to take whatever new leadership book he was just assigned – about Abraham Lincoln, or Kennedy, or maybe Steve Jobs this time – and try to act like that person. Today is the day Bob starts *yet another* round of sudden, sweeping changes across the office in a futile attempt to make Bob appear like the new leader he has just read about.

For a few weeks, Sarah knows, everything in the office will grind to a halt while Sarah and her colleagues try to accommodate this "new" Bob, until, eventually, inevitably, it doesn't work and Bob gives up again, and work can finally return to normal. If only Bob could see what Sarah does:[2]

> *Sarah can see that Bob has spent most of his career striving to be just like the leaders he admires. Yet he fails to realize that the people he looks up to are all very different. There is no single person who embodies even half of the characteristics on Bob's exhaustive list of what makes a well-rounded leader. And perhaps most strikingly, the one leader that Bob knows the least about is* himself.

As a leader, you have to know what your strengths are and how to use them in your job, just as you would as a great employee. If you lose sight of this, you run the risk of   not only failing to become a great leader, but as I explain in the chapter on the Uncanny Valley, of becoming a *terrible* one.

### Managing the best out of your team

While anyone can be a leader, only some will ever be managers. It's important to separate what makes a great manager (someone who gets the most out of their team) from a great leader (someone who finds a way to get things done). In all likelihood, you will need to learn how to be both at some point in your career.

Being a great manager means living with the irony that your managerial success is hardly about you at all, it's actually about something that you may have little control over – your team. A

*great manager is one who gets the best out of the team they are
managing.*

Like it or not, this is how we measure managers. Think about
how you would evaluate a football or basketball coach. You would
judge them based on what they get out of their players. This is a
counterintuitive concept for many managers, because as human
beings we so desperately want *our* work to be about *us.*

Unfortunately, many managers do make the work about them.
"This is what *I* want;" "Give *me* the report tomorrow," "*I* approve
your request for vacation." Me, I, oh my! If that's how you think of
management, I'm sorry, but you're going to be in trouble. Being a
great manager not only means doing your own part – you need to
know your own Center, how to build trust, how to communicate,
etc. – it means teaching your team how to do it as well and putting
*them* in positions to succeed (finding *their* Centers). You need to
help them play to their strengths and take advantage of
opportunities. You have to speak to their passions. And you need
to do this while still performing the *additional* mundane
requirements of management:[3] clearly defining roles and
responsibilities; providing feedback; acknowledging and
rewarding good work; correcting mistakes or issues; and
celebrating success.

As mentioned earlier, management is not leadership, and
leadership is not management, though they are related. You can
be a leader without managing anyone or anything, like a great
sports player who helps lead their team to victory. The great
sports player is a leader but *not* the manager. Likewise, you can be
a manager without truly being a leader – if your job as manager
only calls for you to maintain the status quo, you can be great at
that without being much of a leader at all. And that's ok!

Despite this, management and leadership, together, are
incredibly important to career success, and they rarely succeed
without the other. It is rare to be a great leader, or *sustain* being a

great leader, without being a great manager and vice versa. Those who are great at one but *terrible* at the other often fail to sustain their success. And that's not what you want. So make sure to treat each role accordingly, and be ready to divide the two between two different people if necessary.

### The great managing checklist

Gallup has done the yeoman's work of studying 10 million employee and manager interviews in 114 countries and 41 languages to determine how to be a great manager. Through that research, they have developed a very effective list of twelve elements to refer to (that I have long used) to determine if your staff thinks you are great at managing. The more of these that your staff can answer "yes" to, the better manager you are:[4]

1. *I know what is expected of me at work.*

2. I have the materials and equipment to do my job right.

3. *At work, I have the opportunity to do what I do best every day.*

4. In the last seven days, I have received recognition or praise for doing good work.

5. *My supervisor, or someone at work, seems to care about me as a person.*

6. There is someone at work who encourages my development.

7. *At work, my opinions seem to count.*

8. The mission or purpose of my company makes me feel my job is important.

9. *My associates or fellow employees are committed to doing quality work.*

10. I have a best friend at work.

11. *In the last six months, someone has talked to me about my progress.*

12. This last year, I have had opportunities at work to learn and grow.

## Phil Jackson and great coaching

As one study of professional basketball coaches has shown, you do have quite a bit of control over the career success of those you manage, and probably more than you think. In *Stumbling on Wins*, David Berri and Martin Schmidt found that most coaches (68%) *don't have any noticeable effect at all* on the productivity of their players, a list that includes such renowned basketball names as Pat Riley and Jerry Sloan.[5] None of these famous names were found to have a statistically significant impact on their players' performance.

But some NBA coaches in the study did impact their players' performance – and by quite a bit.

The top two? Phil Jackson, who coached Michael Jordan's Chicago Bulls and Kobe Bryant's Los Angeles Lakers, and the San Antonio Spurs' Gregg Popovich. Together, these two coaches have won a combined 16 NBA championships and nearly 70% of the games that their teams have played. These are the two most successful coaches in modern basketball history, and two of the most successful coaches in all of sports period. After controlling for past player performance and other factors, this study found that any team coached by Jackson or Popovich could expect to win *at least 16 more games* than the team would have won *with any other coach*. Of all the coaches surveyed, Jackson and Popovich had the greatest impact on their players, and were two of just three coaches total whose impacts on their players lasted *beyond* the first year that the player played for them. Jackson and Popovich were truly great coaches because of their ability to bring out great results from their players.

Other studies of the federal workforce emphasize this point as well, and state that your manager may in fact be the most important factor in your career success.[6] So yes, it is possible to affect the performance of those you manage, and you, as a manager, should be judged accordingly.

### The idea disease

If you asked around I'm sure many people would credit the success of great leaders as the result of their having great ideas. After all, what good would Apple CEO Steve Jobs have been if he didn't have the idea for smash-hit products like the iPhone, or the iPad? However, if you asked Apple, you would have gotten a different answer entirely. When Apple was near bankruptcy in the late 1990's there was no shortage of good ideas for new Apple products, many of which made it to market. Instead, Apple leaders credited their 21st-century resurgence to focusing on *fewer* good ideas than they had in the 1990's when they nearly when out of business.  Steve Jobs describes what happened to Apple in the 1990's under the leadership of the CEO that temporarily replaced him, John Sculley:[7]

> *One of the things that really hurt Apple was after I left, John Sculley got a very serious disease. And that disease—I've seen other people get it, too—it's the disease of thinking that a having a great idea is really 90 percent of the work. And if you just tell people, 'here's this great idea,' then of course they can go off and make it happen. The problem with that is that there's a tremendous amount of craftsmanship between having a great idea and having a great product.*

As Apple learned the hard way, having an idea is *only an opportunity*, and not necessarily a great one either. And even if it is a great opportunity, you still need your Center – your opportunity, passion, and your strengths aligned, that craftsmanship Jobs speaks of – to turn your idea into something great.

## How to adapt to different styles of communication[8]

Communication is to leadership as air is to breathing. A leader cannot lead if he or she cannot communicate. Unfortunately, not being able to communicate is all too easy to do. Everyone's been there. You're in an important meeting, trying to make an important point, and you can tell the message isn't getting across. *What's going on?*

It could be that you and your colleagues, or your supervisor, have different styles of communicating. Throughout your career, you'll frequently interact with people whose communication styles are different from yours. Learning how to manage these differences is essential to your career. So, how do you communicate effectively with someone who communicates differently than you do? Do these four things recommended by David Merrill and Roger H. Reid and you are well on your way:[9]

❖ *Step 1: Understand the impression you make.* What kind of style do you have? How do others perceive that style? How can your communication style create stress for others?

❖ *Step 2: Take control of your behavior.* Think of the possible strengths and weaknesses of your style. Which ones could cause miscommunication between you and a coworker? Think of ways to maximize your strengths and play down your weaknesses.

❖ *Step 3: Identify other styles.* Observe your coworker's behavior and how he or she responds to your style. Does he or she tend to ask or tell others to do something? Does he or she display emotions or keep them hidden?

❖ *Step 4: Adapt.* Notice the similarities between your styles. Are there places where you have common ground? Make sure to work these traits into your interactions with your coworker. Next, think about the differences between your styles. Are there any behaviors you can change to better accommodate the preferences of your coworker?

Remember not to take other people's communication styles personally. Like yours, their styles are simply products of their responsiveness and assertiveness and not necessarily reflections of their thoughts and feelings. However, others might very well take your style personally – so think carefully about tailoring your style appropriately, and when in doubt, always be polite.

## Leading change

I remember in my Monetary Theory class a new, controversial idea came up. The response to this new idea from academia was highly negative, though the theory, and the reasons behind it, were sound.

I still remember my professor's response. He supported the new, controversial position, but wasn't at all surprised by the negative response from his students and peers. I asked him why. "Sometimes," he said, "It takes time for new ideas to sink in." I took that lesson to heart. I've learned that if your idea has no support, it's often best to set it aside and go full speed on one that can succeed. Give it time to sink in.

## Take the shot

Alternatively, if you know you can make the idea work, don't be afraid to take the shot, even if not everyone agrees with you. My favorite example is Apple terminating one of its most successful products at the time when it ended the iPod Mini in 2005. Who in their right mind would just kill off a highly successful product? Michael Lopp writes:[10]

> The Mini had a worthy replacement – the flash-based iPod Nano – and it was likely that favorable price points for flash memory were a driving force in the new product. But why not milk [the Mini]? The Mini had been on the market a year and a half and Apple was still having difficulty keeping the Mini in stock. Why kill a best-selling product? I think the reason, and, more importantly, an emerging Apple strategy, was announced as part of the keynote. [CEO] Steve [Jobs] spent multiple slides showing off the

*Mini's competition, and, not surprisingly, it looked a lot like the
Mini. So rather than letting them catch up, he changed the
game.*

Apple knew it had a new, winning idea – the iPod Nano – and
it didn't want the old iPod Mini to stand in its way. And even
though many disagreed with Apple's decision, Apple did it
anyway, and due to its superior technology and lack of
competition from the now-terminated iPod Mini, the Nano
became a huge success in its own right.

Leading change is hard, especially when others disagree with
your direction, as many have with Apple's. John Kotter wrote the
Bible on leading change in his book of the same name, a book
that all aspiring leaders should own a copy of. In *Leading Change*,
Kotter details the following eight-stage process that he believes
leaders must go through to successfully lead change:[11]

- ❖ *Establish a sense of urgency.*
- ❖ *Create the guiding coalition.*
- ❖ *Develop a vision and a strategy.*
- ❖ *Communicate the change vision.*
- ❖ *Empower broad-based action.*
- ❖ *Generate short-term wins.*
- ❖ *Consolidate gains and produce more change.*
- ❖ *Anchor new approaches in the culture.*

These lessons are very important to be aware of because if
you're not leading some sort of change, you're not much of a
leader, are you?

### Dog-fooding

One summer while in college I took on a part-time job for a
local green energy advocacy group. The group's primary mission

was fundraising, and their favorite tactic was to go door-to-door asking for individual donations. They had a script that each employee was supposed to memorize and follow word-for-word when knocking on doors. During one of my training sessions, someone in the group asked why we follow a script at all. Why can't we just say anything we want to? The supervisor of the group said that, in theory, he had no problem with a more free-flowing approach. The problem was they had already tried it. One day, every doorknocker was sent out with no script at all and told to say only whatever they thought would work best in that situation. At the end of the day, the group measured their results using this new, free-flowing method. The results were a miserable failure; the group brought in far fewer donations that day than it expected. The new unscripted method did not perform nearly as well as their scripted method did. Their script, as it turned out, was actually really good.

Having a script can help quite a bit – if your script is really good. I took this lesson to heart and every time I gear up to introduce a change, I do my best to do it myself first. If we are proposing a new training program, I try to deliver the training myself. If we are proposing a new procedure, I try to follow it first, before anyone else does. And so on. This way I can help develop a really good "script" that we can use when it's time to ask the entire group to follow our lead. Companies often call this approach "dog-fooding," which means (somewhat grossly) that if you really want to sell good dog food, you should try eating it first – if it's good enough for you, it's good enough for the dog. This approach, "dog-fooding," not only produces much better results than simply leading by decree, it will also earn you the invaluable respect of your team.

### Culture killers

When you're building a new culture with your team or staff, you have to be aware that not everyone will buy what you're selling. Some people will come around eventually, some never will, and still others will work to kill the new culture you're creating. You have to cut them out.

Jim Collins details this very well in his chapter on "Getting the Right People on the Bus" in *Good to Great*. I have a lot of strategies for this myself. But the basic principle is this: find your core team that shares your vision, spend as much time with them as you can, and concentrate the rest of your time on the slow adopters. Spend as little time as possible with the non-believers, and especially the culture killers. They may be fine people and good for something else. But if you let them into your team and they start tearing it apart, cut them out. They had their chance. Now it's time to move on and accomplish the mission without them.

### Training others

A colleague of mine was working at a hiring fair when a veteran of the U.S. armed forces came to her asking for help in applying to a job. She was happy to oblige, she said. But he didn't know how to use a computer. He didn't even know the basics for turning it on, connecting to the internet, or creating a new document in order to apply. It was sad, she told me, but when she showed him how to do it he understood how and even later showed her that he had learned and remembered what she had taught him. Once he was taught, he learned and adapted very quickly.

While it is relatively rare for many people today to not know how to do computer functions like these, that disconnect between the potential employee's actual skills and what their potential employer really needs is all too common. In my opinion, there is a systemic lack of investment in training across the country.

In my experience in both individual offices and across a large organization, the benefits of up-to-date, high quality, and agile training are immense, and measurably so. But employers are afraid that their employees will take the training and run to another job, so instead they make do with poorly trained staff. That makes absolutely no sense, but chances are you'll have to deal with this too.

I once asked a top executive at a multi-billion dollar federal agency, one who ran one of the most successful organizations in the agency, what the secret to his success was. In so many words, he said that it was in recruiting people with the right attitude, first, and providing them with the right training, second.

A very well-reviewed program I used to run adopted the same secret to success. I invested in a leading recruitment assessment process that provided me with a stream of top talent that others in my agency had not yet found in a structured way. Then, I obtained leading training that was agile and cutting-edge. If you haven't heard of Lynda.com, you should check it out. I believe it (and others like it) is the future of training. In my office, the results spoke for themselves. My staff loved it, and being so well motivated and so highly skilled, they were seen as leaders in our organization, even though their median age was only 25 years old. The average age of our employees, overall? 47 years old.

## Metrics

Metrics are a fascinating topic. They intersect so many key areas in professional success. Incentives. Accountability. Analysis. I think one of the key turning points in the professional growth of a good employee into a great one is understanding metrics.

Metrics in many ways rule all. Critical funding decisions, firing decisions, strategic decisions, virtually anything of importance to your career is in some way decided by metrics, all the way down to how you prioritize your daily work and decide what not to do. Yet they are inherently limited, misused, and often flawed. But because so few can speak the language of metrics these problem areas are often ignored.

I want to focus on only one aspect of metrics initially – how they ought to be used. Metrics serve two roles: First, they are your "scoreboard." They set expectations for what success means to your organization. Second, they are your incentive structure. All behavior will bend towards whatever behavior the metric says is valuable, and critically, against all other behavior, even if that other behavior is itself valuable or even more valuable than the metric.

In a word, metrics can be dangerous.

As a number of leading researchers have pointed out, leading organizations tend to limit their use of metrics. What metrics they do use to measure success tend to be exclusively for the entire organization, not each individual competing part. Apple, for example, does not rank its iPod division against its iPhone with separate metrics. While they measure each division separately, there is only one metric for success – Apple's overall success. So if iPod sales are declining due to, say, rising iPhone sales which are cannibalizing the iPod, that is perfectly ok for Apple since Apple is still growing.

This is not the case for most organizations. In most organizations, when an established service or product is threatened by a new innovation in another office within the same organization, the innovation is stymied. Nearly every large organization has operated this way at some point, and many still do, which is why large organizations so often fail to innovate. This phenomenon is the subject of Clayton Christensen's famous book *The Innovator's Dilemma*. Metrics serve an important goal, but they are only a means to an end. It's up to you to use them appropriately.

### Protect your people

In my first job at VA there was a beloved senior leader who when asked about leadership advice, frequently refrained that in order to lead change, "you have to protect your people." You had to train them, support them, and, when they were being unfairly maligned, defend them too. The effect this had on the people who worked for him, myself included, was profound. You felt like you would run through a wall for him because you knew he depended on you. When you made a mistake, you felt like you let him down personally, and were extremely motivated to never let that happen again. While he was employed there, everyone I knew who worked for him felt the same way. And when he left, none of us ever felt the same way again. We never saw another leader of such high rank personally go to bat for us for training, resources, or simply give us a simple benefit of the doubt in the way that he had. Morale plummeted and was never the same again.

I didn't fully appreciate this lesson until he was gone, and two events happened. First, I felt the brunt end of what it was like to receive criticisms and not have the support of leadership, which was very debilitating. Once you lose support and are left alone to defend against (unfair) criticism, there are days when it feels like there is no point to trying to improve or giving that extra effort, since doing anything new can only expose you to further criticism.

I took that lesson with me and made it a point to protect my team whenever an issue arose in the future so that they would always feel motivated to produce their best work. I would do my best to make sure they had the training and support they needed, and would get a fair hearing if any issues arose or any one leveled criticisms against them. As long as my team did what they needed to keep my trust (i.e. they acted responsibly and gave me their best work), I in turn gave them my full support, made myself available to them when they needed me most, heard them out when I thought they might have any concerns, and gave them the benefit of the doubt when any unsubstantiated criticisms were leveled at them. Your team is full of people with real lives, and often families, that depend on you for their livelihoods; don't ever take that for granted.

### The one rule to rule them all

Leadership is the one thing that can override everything else in your career. Never underestimate the ability of a poor leader to ruin your day, or the ability of a good leader to brighten it. Do you want to know the best way to deal with a poor leader?

Become a good one. They are forever in short supply.

# CONCLUSION

# Beware the Uncanny Valley

In the early 2000s, film studios were eager to capitalize both on the stunning success of the first computer generated animated films, most famously Pixar's *A Toy Story*, as well as the immense power of the next generation of computer technology. In 2001, Square Pictures believed it had the recipe for the next computer generated blockbuster in its animated film *Final Fantasy: The Spirits Within*. Press leading up to its release touted the next-generation quality of its graphics and the incredible amount of detail their characters would have – including rendering individual skin pores, as well as thousands of individual strands of hair on their heads.

Not only was the film a total bust (Square Pictures lost $52 million and was bankrupted), but the excruciating level of detail that went into *Final Fantasy*'s animation actually *hurt* the film.[1] Film critic Jason Vice wrote that, "The film's greatest strength is also one of its biggest weaknesses. As realistic-looking as the characters are, the flat, expressionless features make them seem emotionally aloof and rather unsympathetic."[2] Other film critics described the animation as cold, mechanical, and "creepily artificial."[3]

Three years after the failure of *Final Fantasy* came Pixar's *The Incredibles*. If *Final Fantasy* were the Lamborghini of computer animation, *The Incredibles* would instead be the Ford Focus. Where *Final Fantasy*'s characters had detailed features and blemishes meant to mimic physical reality, *The Incredibles* had rounded curves, flat surfaces, and monochrome colors meant to strip away the barnacles of physical reality.

And it worked. *The Incredibles*' design aesthetic won many plaudits, and the box office returns were, well, incredible – over $444 million in net profits, or nearly $500 million more than *Final Fantasy*.

This was no accident. *The New York Times* wrote:[4]

> Mr. Bird [the creator of the film] decided that to make the characters in 'The Incredibles' more real, he would have to make them less so. Computer animators can now program pores and facial hair into a character's skin, but the outcome isn't necessarily more convincing. Mr. Bird said he wanted to do more with less, 'capturing the essence of reality' rather than 'recreating reality.'

The difference between *Final Fantasy* and *The Incredibles* was, superficially, that one was a huge success and the other a bankrupting failure. But why? Why did it have to be this way? Why was *Final Fantasy*'s amazing breakthrough in technology a *contributor* to its failure, instead of being the harbinger of great success it was intended to be? This other, deeper difference is known as the Uncanny Valley.

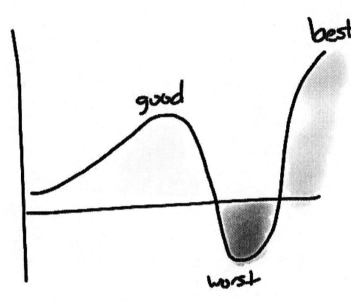

*The Uncanny Valley, by Ben Thompson. Time moves to the right. First you are adequate (the beginning of the curved line), then you become good (the first hump), next you – potentially – become very bad (the big dip), before finally becoming great.*[5]

The Uncanny Valley teaches us that, sometimes, the absolute worst thing you can do is actually the closest thing to being the absolute best – and to go from good to best, you may have to be prepared to go through the worst.

This theory originates from robotics. In the 1970's, a Japanese roboticist noticed something very peculiar about the reaction people had to his robots. People liked it when the robots became more human-like – but only up to a point. A machine with steel "arms" and "legs" was cute, like *The Iron Giant*. But a robot with a human-like face that didn't speak or move *quite* like a human was *revolting*. It was, counter-intuitively, much worse to be *almost* human than it was to be *just a little* human.

Like in robotics, in many tasks it can also be *much worse* to be close to great then it is to be merely good. Many a failed leader has experienced this by falling deep into the Uncanny Valley, never to return, and many people fail to become great because they don't plan for it either. The key to traversing the Uncanny Valley is knowing that it exists, that it can be passed, but that you must prepare for it first.

Could you imagine if you moved into a new home without a plan to get your furniture from point A to point B if you just tried to wing it? It would be terrible, wouldn't it, if it you lost furniture or the new home didn't meet your needs in some way?

Alternatively, what if you did a good job in planning the move to your new home? Isn't that the ultimate best place to be – a nice, simple move into an even better home?

During your move, the "good" part of the process was your old home that you lived in before, the "best" part of the process is your new home that you move into, and the "worst" is the move in between. You go from good, to worst, to best, in that order.

Just because you had to go through the move – the worst part – doesn't mean the move wasn't worth it, does it? It really depends on how well the move went. If the move was a complete disaster – items lost or broken, furniture irreparably damaged – then the move may not have been worth it. Square Pictures' "move" into making movies was so bad that it bankrupted them. But bad moves are preventable, just like the mistakes that Square Pictures made were preventable, if you plan for them.

## Don't get stuck in the valley

The key lesson of the Uncanny Valley is not to be so afraid of the valley that you never strive to be the best. It is that you become aware of the valley, so that you can plan for it, and come through to the other side. If you are conducting a public performance, practice your routine before it goes live. If you're writing a report, read it over or share it with a confidant before you give it to the boss. Research, research, research and practice, practice, practice. Just because you *have* to encounter an Uncanny Valley doesn't mean you *have* to experience disaster, like Square Pictures did.

As you work towards greatness, you will encounter many Uncanny Valleys in your career. Whenever you learn a new skill, take on a new challenge you are unfamiliar with, assume a new leadership role – these all have uncanny valleys. You will have to take a step back with each one before you can take two steps forward.

But don't get stuck in the valley – you can succeed in each one of these challenges if you have a plan to get to the other side.

# Notes

---

## CHAPTER 1. GOOD VS. GREAT

[1] Jim Collins, *Good to Great: Why Some Companies Make the Leap...and Others Don't.* HarperCollins Publishers Inc. (2001), p. 1

[2] *Good to Great*, p.97

[3] *Good to Great*, p. 97

[4] Paul Graham, "What Doesn't Seem Like Work?" January 2015. URL: http://www.paulgraham.com/work.html

[5] *Good to Great*, p. 109

[6] *Good to Great*, p. 110

[7] The Partnership for Public Service, "Ten Years of Best Places to Work Rankings: How Six Federal Agencies Improved," December 18, 2013. URL: http://ourpublicservice.org/publications/viewcontentdetails.php?id=23, p.1

## CHAPTER 2. STRENGTHS: WHAT DO I DO?

[1] Dan Witters, Jim Asplund, and Jim Harter, "Half in U.S. Don't Use Their Strengths throughout the Day," Gallup, September 12, 2012. URL: http://www.gallup.com/poll/157397/half-don-strengths-throughout-day.aspx.

[2] Tom Rath and Barry Conchie, *Strengths Based Leadership: Great Leaders, Teams, and Why People Follow.* Gallup Press (January 2009), p.14-15

[3] *Strengths Based Leadership*, p. xx

[4] *Strengths Based Leadership*, p.16

[5] John D. Bransford et. al, *How People Learn: Brain, Mind, Experience, and School.* National Academy Press (2000), p.117

[6] Adapted from: https://mycareeratva.va.gov/library/career-development-training-courses/training-course-increasing-job-satisfaction.

[7] Steve Jobs, "Computers are like a bicycle for our minds." Michael Lawrence Films. URL: https://www.youtube.com/watch?v=ob_GX50Za6c. Uploaded June 1, 2006.

[8] "Ira Glass on Storytelling, part 3 of 4," Public Radio International. Video: https://www.youtube.com/watch?v=BI23U7U2aUY&feature=youtu.be. Transcript: http://nprfreshair.tumblr.com/post/4931415362/nobody-tells-this-to-people-who-are-beginners-i

## CHAPTER 3. OPPORTUNITY: WHAT'S IN IT FOR ME?

[1] Jack Dennis, "Young adult unemployment is at highest sustained rate since World War II," *Examiner.com*, May 3, 2013. URL: http://www.examiner.com/article/young-adult-unemployment-is-at-highest-sustained-rate-since-world-war-ii

[2] Walter Hamilton, "More than 4 in 5 college seniors don't have jobs lined up," *The Los Angeles Times*, May 7, 2014. URL: http://www.latimes.com/business/la-fi-mo-more-than-4-in-5-college-seniors-dont-have-jobs-lined-up-20140507-story.html

[3] Matthew Reed and Debbie Cochrane, "Student Debt and the Class of 2013." The Project on Student Debt, November 2014. URL: http://projectonstudentdebt.org/files/pub/classof2013.pdf

[4] Nanci Hellmich, "Survey: More employers plan to hire new college grads," *USA Today*, April 30, 2014. URL: http://www.usatoday.com/story/money/personalfinance/2014/04/24/college-graduates-jobs-careerbuilder/8017155/

[5] Richard Fry, "A Rising Share of Young Adults Live in Their Parents' Home," Pew Research Center, August 1, 2013. URL: http://www.pewsocialtrends.org/2013/08/01/a-rising-share-of-young-adults-live-in-their-parents-home/

[6] Thomas Edsall, "Has American Business Lost Its Mojo?" *The New York Times*, April 1, 2015. URL: http://www.nytimes.com/2015/04/01/opinion/thomas-edsall-has-american-business-lost-its-mojo.html?emc=edit_ty_20150401&nl=opinion&nlid=34755528

[7] Spencer Woodman, "Exclusive: Amazon makes even temporary warehouse workers sign 18-month non-competes." *The Verge*, March 26, 2015. URL: http://www.theverge.com/2015/3/26/8280309/amazon-warehouse-jobs-exclusive-noncompete-contracts

[8] Yuval Rosenberg, "The Myth Of The Small-Business Job Engine." *Business Insider*, August 29, 2011. URL: http://www.businessinsider.com/the-myth-of-the-small-business-job-engine-2011-8

[9] Tim Kane, "The Importance of Startups in Job Creation and Job Destruction." *Kauffman Foundation Research Series: Firm Formation and Economic Growth*, July 2010. URL: http://www.kauffman.org/~/media/kauffman_org/research%20reports%20and%20covers/2010/07/firm_formation_importance_of_startups.pdf

[10] Abhijit V. Banerjee and Esther Duflo. *Poor Economics: A Radical Rethinking of the Way to Fight Global Poverty*. PublicAffairs (2012), p. 32

[11] Ibid, p. 33

[12] Ibid.

[13] Ibid.

[14] Yuichi Shoda, Walter Mischel, and Philip K. Peake, "Predicting Adolescent Cognitive and Self-Regulatory Competencies from Preschool Delay of Gratification: Identifying Diagnostic Conditions." *Developmental Psychology* (1990), 26 (6): 978–986. doi:10.1037/0012-1649.26.6.978.

[15] C.R., "NIMBYs in the twenty-first century." *The Economist*, March 25, 2015. URL: http://www.economist.com/blogs/freeexchange/2015/03/wealth-inequality?fsrc=scn/tw/te/bl/ed/nimbysinthetwentyfirstcentury

[16] Peter Sims, *Little Bets: How Breakthrough Ideas Emerge from Small Discoveries*. Free Press (2011), p.1

[17] *Little Bets*, p.13-14

[18] Jena McGregor, "How cleaning the office coffee pot could help protect your job." *The Washington Post*, February 17, 2015. URL:

http://www.washingtonpost.com/blogs/on-leadership/wp/2015/02/17/how-cleaning-out-the-coffee-pot-at-work-could-help-protect-you-from-a-layoff/?tid=sm_tw

[19] Wikipedia. URL: http://en.wikipedia.org/wiki/Abraham_Maslow

[20] Stephen M.R. Covey and Rebecca Merrill, *The Speed of Trust: The One Thing That Changes Everything.* Free Press (2005), p.3

[21] *The Speed of Trust*, p. xxii

[22] Frederic Luskin, Ph.D. Rick Aberman, Ph.D. Arthur E. DeLorenzo, Sr.; "Effect of Training of Emotional Competence in Financial Services Advisors." Consortium for Research on Emotional Intelligence in Organizations (2005). URL: http://www.eiconsortium.org/reports/emotional_competence_training_financial_advisors.

[23] Wikipedia. URL: http://en.wikipedia.org/wiki/Hanlon%27s_razor

[24] Joel Osteen, April 20, 2015. URL: https://twitter.com/JoelOsteen/status/590210901552300032

[25] Adapted from: http://www.mycareeratva.va.gov/library/career-development-training-courses/training-course-increasing-job-satisfaction.

## CHAPTER 4. PASSION: WHO AM I?

[1] Alice Muellerweiss, *It's Your Career: Own It!* Charles Pinot (2014), p.39

[2] Shawn Anchor, "The Happy Secret to Better Work." May 2011. Video: http://www.ted.com/talks/shawn_achor_the_happy_secret_to_better_work

[3] Ibid.

[4] Sarah Kliff, "Want to increase your productivity? Study says: Look at this adorable kitten." *The Washington Post*, October 1, 2012. URL: http://www.washingtonpost.com/blogs/wonkblog/wp/2012/10/01/want-to-increase-your-productivity-study-says-look-at-this-adorable-kitten/

[5] Alex Palmer, "Study: Workplace Music Boosts Productivity." *IncentiveMag.com*, July 5, 2012. URL: http://www.incentivemag.com/News/Industry/Study--Workplace-Music-Boosts-Productivity/

[6] Jennifer Valentino-Devries, "Steve Jobs's Best Quotes." *The Wall Street Journal*, August 24, 2011. URL: http://blogs.wsj.com/digits/2011/08/24/steve-jobss-best-quotes/

[7] Barry Schwartz, "The Paradox of Choice." July 2005. Video: http://www.ted.com/talks/barry_schwartz_on_the_paradox_of_choice

[8] Adapted from: https://mycareeratva.va.gov/library/career-development-training-courses/training-course-increasing-job-satisfaction.

[9] Adapted from https://mycareeratva.va.gov/library/career-development-training-courses/training-course-increasing-job-satisfaction.

[10] Travis Bradberry, "All the reasons why emotionally intelligent people are so happy at work." *Government Executive*, March 23, 2015. URL: http://www.govexec.com/excellence/promising-practices/2015/03/all-reasons-why-emotionally-intelligent-people-are-so-happy-work/108169/?oref=govexec_today_pm_nl

## CHAPTER 5. THE PLAN

[1] "StrengthsFinder Themes," *StrengthsTest.com*. URL: http://www.strengthstest.com/strengthsfinderthemes/strengths-themes.html

[2] Ibid.

[3] Ibid.

[4] Ibid.

[5] Ibid.

[6] David DiSalvo, "Visualize Success if You Want to Fail." *Forbes*, June 8, 2011. URL: http://www.forbes.com/sites/daviddisalvo/2011/06/08/visualize-success-if-you-want-to-fail/

[7] *CareerInfoNet.org*. URL: http://www.careerinfonet.org/oview3.asp?printer=&next=oview3&level=Overall&optstatus=&id=1&nodeid=5&soccode=&stfips=00&jobfam=&group=1&showall=no

[8] Mike Monterio, "F--- You, Pay Me." URL: http://vimeo.com/22053820

[9] Mike Monteiro, *Design Is a Job*. A Book Apart (2012). URL: http://www.amazon.com/Design-Is-Job-Mike-Monteiro/dp/1937557049

[10] Adapted from: http://www.mycareeratva.va.gov/library/individual-development-plan-idp/tips-planning-successful-idp-conversation

[11] James Surowiecki, *The Wisdom of Crowds*. Anchor (August 2005), p. xiii

## CHAPTER 6. THE ROUTINE

[1] Stephen R. Covey, *The 7 Habits of Highly Effective People: Powerful Lessons in Personal Change*. Free Press (2004), p. 18

[2] *The 7 Habits of Highly Effective People*, p. 19

[3] *The 7 Habits of Highly Effective People*, p. 35

[4] Ronald A. Howard and Clinton D. Korver, *Ethics for the Real World: Creating a Personal Code to Guide Decisions in Work and Life*. Harvard Business Review Press (2008).

[5] Tjare A. Tjambolang, "The Impact of the Office Environment on Employee Productivity," p.1. URL: https://www.yumpu.com/en/document/view/4449170/1-the-impact-of-the-office-environment-on-employee-

[6] Stephanie Lichtenfeld, Andrew J. Elliot, Markus A. Maier, and Reinhard Pekrun, "Fertile Green: Green Facilitates Creative Performance." Pers Soc Psychol Bull, June 2012; vol. 38, 6: pp. 784-797. URL: http://psp.sagepub.com/content/38/6/784.abstract

[7] Wyon DP, "The effects of indoor air quality on performance and productivity." US National Library of Medicine, 2004, 14 Suppl 7:92-101. URL: http://www.ncbi.nlm.nih.gov/pubmed/15330777

[8] Bronwyn Fryer, "Sleep Deficit: The Performance Killer." Harvard Business Review, October 2006. URL: https://hbr.org/2006/10/sleep-deficit-the-performance-killer

## CHAPTER 7. DO I NEED A MENTOR? A PARTNER?

[1] Rodd Wagner and Gale Muller, *The Power of 2: How to Make the Most of Your Partnerships at Work and In Life*. Gallup Press (November 2009), p. 4

[2] *The Power of 2*, p. 4-5

[3] *The Power of 2*, p.8-10

# Notes

[4] Adapted from: https://mycareeratva.va.gov/library/mentoring/benefits-mentoring

## CHAPTER 8. HEALTH

[1] *It's Your Career*, p.46-47

[2] Stephen Ilardi, *The Depression Cure: The 6-Step Program to Beat Depression without Drugs*. Da Capo Lifelong Books (June 2010), p. 4

[3] *The Depression Cure*, p. 9

[4] *It's Your Career*, p. 50

[5] Cathy Hayes, "How Bill O'Reilly got healthy - Fox host sheds weight by following 'Wheat Belly' book." IrishCentral.com, August 2, 2012. URL: http://www.irishcentral.com/news/-how-bill-oreilly-got-healthy-fox-host-sheds-weight-by-following-wheat-belly-book-video-164707656-237518911.html

[6] The original appears to not be available online so I have uploaded the recorded excerpts to www.careertalkbook.com; contact me for the URL.

[7] Gordon MacAulay and Grain Growers, "What the world wants from Australian wheat." Australian Government Grains Research and Development Corporation, September 13, 2011. URL: http://www.grdc.com.au/Research-and-Development/GRDC-Update-Papers/2011/09/What-the-world-wants-from-Australian-wheat

[8] Bariatric Surgery Source, "Child Obesity Statistics & Teenage Obesity Statistics: 1963 to Present." URL: http://www.bariatric-surgery-source.com/child-obesity-statistics.html

[9] Bonnie Berkowitz and Patterson Clark, "Don't just sit there!" The Washington Post. URL: http://www.washingtonpost.com/wp-srv/special/health/sitting/Sitting.pdf

## CHAPTER 9. HOW DO I SAVE TIME?

[1] Dave Crenshaw, "Understanding the consequences of multitasking." *Lynda.com*, October 19, 2011. URL: http://www.lynda.com/Entourage-tutorials/Understanding-consequences-multitasking/77533/82350-4.html

[2] Adapted from Dave Crenshaw's *Time Management Fundamentals*, available at Lynda.com. You should take the entire course! URL: http://www.lynda.com/Entourage-tutorials/Understanding-consequences-multitasking/77533/82350-4.html

[3] As quoted by George Musser in "Time on the Brain: How You Are Always Living in the Past, and Other Quirks of Perception," *Scientific American*, September 15, 2011. URL: http://blogs.scientificamerican.com/observations/2011/09/15/time-on-the-brain-how-you-are-always-living-in-the-past-and-other-quirks-of-perception/

[4] Wikipedia. URL: http://en.wikipedia.org/wiki/Flash_lag_illusion

[5] Arzaan, "You Live in the Past/The Flash Lag Effect," *Arzaan's Science Journals*, March 22, 2013. URL: http://arzaanssciencejournals.blogspot.com/2013/03/you-live-in-pastthe-flash-lag-effect.html

[6] David Eagleman as quoted by Burkhard Bilger in *The New Yorker*, April 25, 2011. URL: http://www.newyorker.com/magazine/2011/04/25/the-possibilian.

[7] J.S. Nairne, "Roddy Roediger's Memory" in J. S. Nairne (Ed.), *The foundations of remembering: Essays in honor of Henry L. Roediger, III* (2007). New York: Psychology Press http://www1.psych.purdue.edu/~nairne/pdfs/44.pdf

[8] H. L. Roediger and K. B. McDermott, "Creating false memories: Remembering words not presented in lists." *Journal of Experimental Psychology: Learning, Memory and Cognition* (1995), 21, 803–814. URL: http://memory.wustl.edu/Pubs/1995_Roediger.pdf

[9] Roediger, H.L., Meade, M.L., & Bergman, E.T., "Social contagion of memory." *Psychonomic Bulletin and Review* (2001), 8(2), 365–371.

[10] Benjamin Weiser, "In New Jersey, Rules Are Changed on Witness IDs." *The New York Times*, August 24, 2011. URL: http://www.nytimes.com/2011/08/25/nyregion/in-new-jersey-rules-changed-on-witness-ids.html?_r=0

[11] George Musser, "Time on the Brain: How You Are Always Living In the Past, and Other Quirks of Perception." *Scientific American*, September 15, 2011. URL: http://blogs.scientificamerican.com/observations/2011/09/15/time-on-the-brain-how-you-are-always-living-in-the-past-and-other-quirks-of-perception/

[12] Ibid.

[13] Atul Gawande, *The Checklist Manifesto*. Picador (January 2011). Kindle edition, p. 11

## CHAPTER 10. HOW DO I WRITE A RESUME?

[1] Peg Tyre, "The Writing Revolution." *The Atlantic*, September 19, 2012. URL: http://www.theatlantic.com/magazine/archive/2012/10/the-writing-revolution/309090/

[2] William Zinsser, *On Writing Well, 30th Anniversary Edition: The Classic Guide to Writing Nonfiction*. Harper Perennial (May 2006), p. 7

[3] Wikipedia. URL: http://en.wikipedia.org/wiki/Inverted_pyramid

[4] *On Writing Well*, p. 5

[5] Chip and Dan Heath, *Made to Stick: Why Some Ideas Survive and Others Die.* Random House (2007), p. 75

[6] *Made to Stick*, p.75-76

[7] Adapted from: https://mycareeratva.va.gov/library/resumes/training-course-resume-preparation

[8] Adapted from: http://www.wikihow.com/Sample/Bank-Teller-Cover-Letter.

## CHAPTER 11. HOW DO I ACE MY INTERVIEW?

[1] Adapted from: https://mycareeratva.va.gov/library/interviews/training-course-interview-prep

[2] Adapted from: https://mycareeratva.va.gov/library/networking/training-course-introduction-elevator-pitch-preparation

[3] Thomas H. Neale and Dana Ely, "Speechwriting in Perspective: A Brief Guide to Effective and Persuasive Communication," CRS Report for Congress. Updated April 17, 2007. URL: http://www.au.af.mil/au/awc/awcgate/crs/98-170.pdf, p. 19

[4] Ibid, p. 2

[5] Ibid, p. 19

# Notes

[6] James Herbert, "Landing a punch on Michael Jordan." ESPN.com, September 23, 2013. URL: http://espn.go.com/blog/truehoop/post/_/id/61933/landing-a-punch-on-michael-jordan

[7] Joann Lublin, "Arguing with the Boss: A Winning Career Strategy," *The Wall Street Journal*, August 9, 2012. URL: http://www.wsj.com/articles/SB10000872396390443991704577579201122821724

## CHAPTER 12. SHOULD I NETWORK? ONLINE?

[1] David Brooks, "The Heart Grows Smarter." *The New York Times*, November 5, 2012. URL: http://www.nytimes.com/2012/11/06/opinion/brooks-the-heart-grows-smarter.html?_r=0&hp=&adxnnl=1&adxnnlx=1420052684-j6TpraSKdXDfOPVQ40P8/A

[2] Adapted from: https://mycareeratva.va.gov/sites/default/files/Map%20Your%20Connections%20Worksheet.v1.pdf

[3] Adapted from: http://career-advice.monster.com/job-search/professional-networking/Informational-Interviewing/article.aspx

[4] Tom Rath and Donald Clifton, *How Full Is Your Bucket? Positive Strategies for Work and Life*. Gallup Press (2004). Skillsoft ebook edition. Chapter Two, p. 3

[5] N Wager, G Fieldman, and T Hussey, "The effect on ambulatory blood pressure of working under favourably and unfavourably perceived supervisors." *Occup Environ Med* 2003;60:468-474 doi:10.1136/oem.60.7.468. URL: http://oem.bmj.com/content/60/7/468.abstract

[6] *How Full Is Your Bucket?*, Introduction, p. 2

[7] Adapted from http://mycareeratva.va.gov/library/networking/seven-steps-optimizing-your-linkedin-presence

[8] Kami Dimitrova, "Justine Sacco, Fired After Tweet on AIDS in Africa, Issues Apology." *ABC News*, December 22, 2013. URL: http://abcnews.go.com/International/justine-sacco-fired-tweet-aids-africa-issues-apology/story?id=21301833

[9] Alison Vingiano, "This Is How a Woman's Offensive Tweet Became The World's Top Story." *BuzzFeed*, December 21, 2013. URL: http://www.buzzfeed.com/alisonvingiano/this-is-how-a-womans-offensive-tweet-became-the-worlds-top-s#.bkVd17wGn

[10] Ibid.

[11] See: http://www.wired.com/2012/08/apple-amazon-mat-honan-hacking/ and: http://www.wired.com/2012/08/mat-honan-data-recovery/all/.

## CHAPTER 13. GOING (BACK) TO SCHOOL

[1] Henry L. Roediger III, "How Tests Make Us Smarter." *The New York Times*, July 18, 2014. URL: http://www.nytimes.com/2014/07/20/opinion/sunday/how-tests-make-us-smarter.html?_r=0

[2] Ibid.

[3] Ibid.

[4] Ibid.

5 Joshua Foer, "Secrets of a Mind-Gamer." *The New York Times*, February 15, 2011. URL: http://www.nytimes.com/interactive/2011/02/20/magazine/mind-secrets.html?_r=2&

6 Ibid.

7 Ibid.

8 Ibid.

9 Although I used this technique before reading it some credit for how this concept evolved goes to Robert Miller's excellent preparatory book *Law School Confidential: A Complete Guide to the Law School Experience.*

10 Jeffrey J. Selingo, "Forget Harvard and Stanford. It really doesn't matter where you go to college." *The Washington Post*, March 16, 2015. URL: http://www.washingtonpost.com/news/grade-point/wp/2015/03/16/forget-harvard-and-stanford-it-really-doesnt-matter-where-you-go-to-college/?tid=sm_tw

11 http://www.wsj.com/articles/SB10001424052748704554104575435563989873060

12 Jacquelyn Smith, "The Best and Worst Master's Degree for Jobs." *Forbes*, June 8, 2012. URL: http://www.forbes.com/sites/jacquelynsmith/2012/06/08/the-best-and-worst-masters-degrees-for-jobs-2/

## CHAPTER 14. WHAT IF...

1 *RollingStone.com*. URL: http://www.rollingstone.com/music/artists/madonna/biography.

2 Zack O'Malley Greenburg, "Madonna's Net Worth: $500 Million In 2013." *Forbes*, September 18, 2013. URL: http://www.forbes.com/sites/zackomalleygreenburg/2013/09/18/madonnas-net-worth-500-million-in-2013/

3 Documentary film, *Madonna: Truth or Dare* (1991). Directed by Alek Keshishian, distributed by Miramax Films North America.

4 Jonathan Valania, "The Mouth That Roared: Q&A with Comedian Bill Burr, The Man Who Told Philadelphia to Go F*ck Itself, Hard, And Lived to Tell." *The Huffington Post*, January 23, 2014. URL: http://www.huffingtonpost.com/jonathan-valania/the-mouth-that-roared-qa-_b_4242841.html

5 Ibid.

6 Ibid.

7 Ibid.

8 Lawrence H. Summers, "Remarks at NBER Conference on Diversifying the Science & Engineering Workforce." January 14, 2005. URL: https://web.archive.org/web/20080130023006/http://www.president.harvard.edu/speeches/2005/nber.html

9 Sarah-Jane Leslie, Andrei Cimpian, Meredith Meyer, and Edward Freeland, "Expectations of brilliance underlie gender distributions across academic disciplines." *Science* 16 January 2015: Vol. 347 no. 6219 pp. 262-265 DOI: 10.1126/science.1261375. URL: http://www.sciencemag.org/content/347/6219/262.full

10 Malcolm Gladwell, *Outliers: The Story of Success*. Back Bay Books (June 2011), p. 239-245

11 *Outliers*, p. 245

# Notes

[12] *Outliers*, p. 246

[13] *Outliers*, p. 255-257

## CHAPTER 15. LEADERSHIP

[1] As told by Adam Lashinsky in "The decade of Steve: How Apple's imperious, brilliant CEO transformed American business." *Fortune*, November 5, 2009. URL: "http://archive.fortune.com/2009/11/04/technology/steve_jobs_ceo_decade.fortune/index.htm

[2] *Strengths Based Leadership*, p.7-10

[3] Glenn Llopis, "6 Ways Successful Teams Are Built To Last." *Forbes*, URL: http://www.forbes.com/sites/glennllopis/2012/10/01/6-ways-successful-teams-are-built-to-last/

[4] Rodd Wagner and James K. Harter, "12: The Elements of Great Managing." *Gallup Press* (2006). URL: http://www.gallup.com/press/176450/elements-great-managing.aspx
http://www.gallup.com/press/176450/elements-great-managing.aspx

[5] David Berri and Martin Schmidt, *Stumbling On Wins: Two Economists Expose the Pitfalls on the Road to Victory in Professional Sports*. FT Press (March 2010), Kindle edition loc. 847

[6] The Partnership for Public Service, "Ten Years of Best Places to Work Rankings: How Six Federal Agencies Improved," December 18, 2013. URL: http://ourpublicservice.org/publications/viewcontentdetails.php?id=23, p.1

[7] Chris Foresman, "Steve Jobs on programming, craftsmanship, software, and the Web." *Ars Technica*, July 7, 2012. URL: http://arstechnica.com/apple/2012/07/steve-jobs-on-programming-craftsmanship-software-and-the-web/

[8] Adapted from: http://www.mycareeratva.va.gov/whatsnew/2014/06/05/how-adapt-different-styles-communication

[9] Merrill, David W. and Roger H. Reid. *Personal Styles and Effective Performance*. Florida: CRC Press LLC (1981)

[10] *Randsinrepose.com*, "Someone is coming to eat you." June 28, 2012. URL: http://randsinrepose.com/archives/someone-is-coming-to-eat-you/

[11] John P. Kotter, *Leading Change*. Harvard Business Review Press (1996), p. 21

## CONCLUSION: BEWARE THE UNCANNY VALLEY

[1] Matthew Butler and Lucie Joschko, "Final Fantasy or The Incredibles: Ultra-realistic animation, aesthetic engagement and the uncanny valley." *Animation Studies – Animated Dialogues, 2007*, p.58. URL: http://journal.animationstudies.org/wp-content/uploads/2009/07/ASADArt8MButlerLJoschko.pdf,

[2] Ibid, p. 58

[3] Ibid.

[4] John Canemaker, "A Part-Human, Part-Cartoon Species." *The New York Times*, October 3, 2004. URL: http://www.nytimes.com/2004/10/03/movies/03cane.html

[5] Ben Thompson, "The Uncanny Valley of a Functional Organization." *Stratechery.com*, July 16, 2013. URL: http://stratechery.com/2013/the-uncanny-valley-of-a-functional-organization/